In His Hands

reclaiming your life after tragedy

In His Hands

reclaiming your life after tragedy

AMBASSADOR INTERNATIONAL
GREENVILLE, SOUTH CAROLINA & BELFAST, NORTHERN IRELAND

In His Hands
reclaiming your life after tragedy

Cover design & page layout by A&E Media — David Siglin

ISBN 978 1 932307 98 6

Published by the Ambassador Group

Ambassador Emerald International
427 Wade Hampton Blvd.
Greenville, SC 29609 USA
www. emeraldhouse.com

and

Ambassador Publications Ltd.
Providence House
Ardenlee Street
Belfast BT6 8QJ
Northern Ireland
www. ambassador-productions.com

The colophon is a trademark of Ambassador

This book is published in association with
Patti M. Hummel, President & Agent
The Benchmark Group LLC, Nashville, TN
benchmarkgroup1@aol.com

About the Author

Leslie Ostrander is a speaker and writer who lives her life out loud!

In 1979, at age four, Leslie was a survivor of a fatal car accident. Her life was changed in that instant! Paralyzed from the waist down with a spinal cord injury, Leslie had to grow up as a child confined to a wheelchair. Her vocal cords were also damaged with scar tissue diminishing her voice. Only able to speak in a slight whisper, she was forced to look deep within herself to find the strength to become a woman of substance.

Leslie demonstrates how to rise above adversity and live life with conviction. She shares through her experiences that fear is an emotion that can disable and immobilize. Negative tendencies create bondage far greater than the paralysis she faces everyday. She has the ability to get people to examine their own limitations and provides life application skills that can help others reach their greatest potential.

In His Hands is a story of hope that will move you to tears and laughter. Share in this journey of discovery and experience the power of faith. Capture and utilize the uplifting attitude that Leslie uses to overcome injury, tragedy, and despair. Discover the foundation she has found, propelling her to victory in pageantry, life, and love.

Leslie is married to her best friend, Aaron and is the adoring mother of two.

For speaking engagements or booking information, contact Leslie at www.lesliespeaks.com or call 706.888.7253.

Dedicated to my children

When adversity knocks on your door, how will you respond? Will you choose to see your own adversities as stepping stones or see them as hurdles? Will you put faith and trust into action? These things alone determine if you will become a victim of circumstance or a conqueror.

— Leslie

Table of Contents

Foreword

I was told my writing was not personal enough. I needed to adapt my writing style to showcase 'me' more. "After all, it is an autobiography you are writing," a friend suggested. I was not discouraged by my friend's unenthusiastic response. Yet, his words made me question my ability to express my thoughts. Had I not conveyed a message more powerful than the style in which it was written? Was my choice of words and sentence structure a distraction from my passion to share my testimony?

I can agree that I am not the next Ernest Hemingway, nor do I wish to become a literary legacy. I only aspire to share my adversities, suffering, and blessings to honor The One who has carried me through.

I've also been told that my writing does not need to be preachy or persuasive. However, I can't take Jesus out of my story because He is the story. "Stay neutral." a literary agent once instructed me. My point: I could be the worst writer to inscribe on a blank sheet of paper, but God gave me the enthusiasm and ability to change this white space into a story, a message that I believe no matter how it is written, holds the potential to change and heal broken spirits. God gave me fingers to type, a mind to create, and a life worthy of sharing. My intentions are to do my best to portray the strength I have found in Him. With the help of the Holy Spirit, hopefully content will overshadow my inexperience in writing. I have a passion to spread the love I have found in Jesus Christ and feel that this ministry is so important, that I must pursue it at all costs. The fulfillment of God's plan for my life is at stake.

This is me; no hidden agenda, no drama added. This is not my story, but one about a life that was created by His hands. A life compared to a waltz — a classical dance — where God and I move hand in hand. God has given me *A Gift*, and gifts are to be shared.

*"I want to empower people to see beyond limitations
and to discover life's unexpected gifts."*
-Leslie

Angels

A radiating sharp pain engulfed my back and shot into my head. A cramp in my spine surfaced. Surprisingly I could feel everything! I thought to myself, *the irony of it all.* For the majority of my life, I had been denied the pleasure of sensation in over one third of my body, and now, immense pain, like no pain I had felt before. The contractions started high in my abdomen and branched out covering my lower back. They continued and were only two minutes apart, progressively getting stronger. The anesthesiologist rolled me over on my side and asked my husband and mother to leave the room. "Can't someone stay with me?" I asked. "I need someone with me." I began to cry. I gripped the side rail of the hospital bed tightly and bit my lower lip with a grimace. The next contraction consumed my entire body. Compared to wave on a hostile sea, the pain started out slowly and gradually increased to unbearable anguish. I thought to myself, *I will never make it through this.*

As I beseeched for relief, I glanced down at my left knee. A small scar caught my attention — a disfigurement that instantly transformed my thoughts to a different time and distant place.

The burn of the scuff was intense. Rich, red blood covered my entire knee. My grandmother was there to mend my wound. She knelt to the ground and removed a handkerchief from her purse, then applied pressure. "Sweetheart," she said, "you need to slow down. We have plenty of time to enjoy the day. Let's try to make it through the day with no more falls." With one hand on my knee and the other on my cheek, she leaned forward and gently kissed my forehead. She brushed my hair from my eyes and wiped away my tears. "You're my girl." She smiled and sat down beside me with her hand still upon my wounded knee.

I was in full labor and about to give birth to my firstborn. This unfamiliar situation terrified me. Never had I experienced such a spectrum of emotions. There was fear and uncertainty combined with severe pain. These emotions were shared with absolute excitement and anticipation. I also had the identical protective feeling that my grandmother had given me the day I fell. As the doctor progressed with the epidural, Aaron held my hand. The team of physicians and nurses proceeded to prep me for the cesarean section. I secretly prayed, *Jesus, I know I shouldn't ask but I need to know that everything is going to be fine.* I knew I was to rely on my faith, but in this particular moment I needed a little reassurance. A little gift of peace was all I was asking for.

 A nurse came to the bedside and introduced herself, "Hi, Leslie. My name is Dot and I will be with you the entire time." With those simple words, I knew my prayer had been answered. Dot was my grandmother's name. There had been several gentle reminders of her since I went into labor that morning. And now another gift of peace came to me in a nurse who shared my grandmother's name.

I had always imagined my grandmother as my guardian angel. In this moment, the sound of her name alone gave me a sense of peace. Aaron kissed my hand. "Honey, they are about to start. Are you doing alright?" I nodded as I struggled to restrain the tears. It only took minutes. The room was filled with this strange yet amazing squall of a newborn's cry. "Congratulations. It's a boy," Dr. Fernandez announced. She was holding this small purple and blue child who was no bigger than a five pound bag of sugar. Instantly I fell in love. It was 4:04 in the afternoon, and I knew my life would never be the same again.

Aaron made his way over to our new son who was wrapped tightly in a warm swaddling blanket. Aaron carried him over to me. He was so little that the blanket swallowed his miniature body. I reached inside the blanket to touch him for the first time and gave him his first kiss. It was a remarkable moment that will forever be etched in my mind.

Dylan was four weeks early. The physicians wanted to observe him for the first few hours. I wanted Aaron to be there with him. With no hesitation, as any good father would, Aaron left me in the care of the surgical team and carried our son to the nursery. I still wanted someone to be by my side. I asked for Dot, the nurse. The anesthesiologist was the closest to me, and he called for her. I was weak and my voice was nothing more than a whisper. Had I tried to call for the nurse, it would have been impossible to be heard above the clamor of activity. He called once more. No response. "Mrs. Ostrander," he asked, "what did the nurse look like?" I responded, "She is a petite black woman. She reassured me that she would be with me through the surgery." He looked around the room once more and replied, "I'm afraid that there has never been a nurse on your surgical team who fits that description."

I lay there and wondered. *Was she really an angel? Was my grandmother watching over me? Was Dot the gift of peace I had asked for?*

August 17, 1979

*For it is by grace you have been saved, through faith — and this
not from yourselves, it is the gift of God.*
Ephesians 2:8

It was the summer of 1979 and I was taking pleasure in our annual family vacation. I was no more than four. With a stance of a prowling tiger, I was eager for the football to be passed to me. In one fluid motion, my father tossed the ragged football my way. I ran with a gunfighter's swagger. The oversized jersey hung well below my knees, making it virtually impossible for me not to fall. My long blonde hair swung from side to side. I sprinted to a thin white chalk line that marked the end zone. With my signature leap over the score line, I spiked the ball and celebrated the way any child would.

Three-year-old Leslie.

After our game of football, my sister and I got our bikes and rode to the corner store. The store had been there since the Great Depression. It had been best known as a stopover for people anxious to get somewhere else. The few cottages within a mile of the store were only reserved by those hardy enough to spend a week at the beach in un-air-conditioned comfort (or lack of). But for us, the wholesome culture and natural slice of beach was our little piece of heaven.

As we walked into the store the same clerk who had greeted my sister year after year greeted us with a smile. "Welcome back," he said. He knew she had been there season after season. My sister retrieved a list from her

Four-year-old Leslie playing out-doors, early in summer, 1979.

back pocket. Aisle by aisle my sister picked each item: sugar, coffee, eggs, bread, and then one last stop to the upright cooler in the front of the store. Reaching inside she inspected the two half-pint plastic containers, smiled, and selected one. The clerk complimented her selection, a carton of fresh raw oysters. "Folks around here will tell you that our oysters are the best anywhere," he said. With a slight grin, my sister replied "Oh I know, we eat them every time we come to the beach."

I waltzed up to the counter, reaching into my pocket for a quarter. "One rainbow ice cream for the young lady," the grey haired clerk said. He winked his eye, and in a southern Cajun voice said, "Now, ya'll come back." I paused for a moment. I'm sure with a look of inquisitiveness. I found this man fascinating and his deep southern expression sounded strange and stirred my curiosity. But the tasty treats we

This photo was taken one week before the tragic day. I am standing with my mother, Judy, my great-grandmother, Granny Olive, and my grandmother, Dot, who I called Muner.

had purchased beckoned for my attention. I took pleasure in eating the rainbow pop. Hastily attempting to consume it before the summer's heat turned it into a melted mess. The ice cream was one of my favorites; however, I simply could not wait to get into those oysters.

We placed the brown paper bags in the front baskets of our bikes and peddled back to our cottage. With no waste of time, we took the half-pint container of oysters, saltine crackers, and ketchup and headed for the front swing on the porch. Side by side, my sister and I laughed as the juice from the salty shellfish ran down our chins. The cool sea breeze air blew the hinged screen door back and forth.

Prepared and ready for a new day of adventure, I awoke with an odd feeling. My vision was distorted. My head was encased in excruciating pain, and the noises seemed so far away. I felt like I was in a deep hole. Slightly awake, I struggled to distinguish my surroundings. I was confused. I could perceive that my left leg was in some type of device and my right leg seemed to have just vanished. There were metal wires and plaster hinging my joints together, forcing my body into one restrictive position. *Where was I and how did I get here?* My confusion intensified. With every ounce of energy, I tried to move my toes. Nothing. Not even a slight movement. I tried again. I could not comprehend what had happened. I knew my body had physically changed. Something was dreadfully wrong. No one had to explain. It was evident. I was broken.

Before I awoke in the hospital, a trauma doctor had concluded my diagnosis of C-7 quadriplegic, *incomplete,* as if somehow fate had forgotten to finish the job. I was in the Pediatric Intensive Care Unit in Opelika, Alabama. There was never a horrifying scream, just disturbing confusion of displacement when I first came out of unconsciousness, an obscure dull kind of uncertainty. It was almost as though I knew my body had changed while I had been asleep. I had no feeling below my waist. My mouth was dry, and my throat engrossed with pressure. My nose was filled with sear-

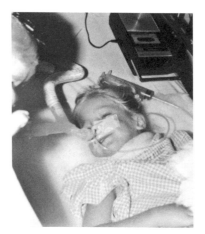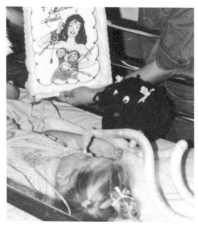

Just days after the accident, I lay in ICU with a respirator and the cassette recorder, my sole method of communication with my mother.

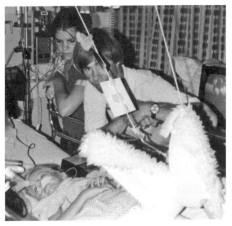

My leg is stabilized by traction, a pulling force to reduce fracture and maintain bone alignment.

ing pain. I was aware of a tube inserted in my nostrils that continued down my throat. Rhythmic beeps and whistles, alarms, and monitors surrounded me. I tried to lift my head with no success. I rotated my eyes as far down as possible to see what was restricting my body from moving. I recognized nothing.

For the next thirty days I would be in and out of a conscious state. I would try hastily, each time I awoke, to figure out how and why, desperately attempting each time to move my toes. My broken body lay in its paralyzed state, motionless. Day by day, I battled the physical pain and drug-induced sedation, searching for some sign of hope. I was young, but in a fight for my life. I was forced into an unrecognizable place where my childhood was stripped away — stolen — along with the movement of my legs. There was a feeling of finality.

The first twenty-four hours after my injury, my life hinged between heaven and hell. Constant monitoring of my depressed respiratory system revealed that a ventilator was necessary. It would ensure that my next breath would come. Although my memory is vague, I will never forget the gift of peace that was given to me that day.

The hospital room was filled with people. The doctor instructed me, "You're going to have to open your mouth real big." I was beyond scared. I silently screamed from within, begging God to help me understand what was happening. *Where are my parents?* With tears running down my face, I trembled with fear. A nurse began to rub my forehead and sweetly sang,

'All things bright and beautiful,
All creatures big and small,
All things wise and wonderful,
The Lord God made them all.'

20

Somehow I knew they were trying to help me. I did my best to settle my fears and listen carefully as I was instructed what to do. I fixed my eyes upon the nurse, who was only a stranger to me, but her voice was the only thing that offered comfort. She continued to sing,

'Each little flower that opens,
Each little bird that sings,
God made their glowing colors,
And He made their tiny wings.'

Peace came upon me. The doctors later told my father of their amazement. The cooperation I gave was more than what would be expected of a young child. Most children would require anesthesia. In my situation, respiratory failure was certain, and sedation could be fatal. Although my respiratory system had been saved now, my cardiovascular system was at risk from the effects of the drugs given for intubations.

For the moment my life had been spared. My heart was physically weak, but it had spiritually changed. With my first breath from the ventilator, I was transformed. This profound moment was unmistakably marked by the presence of Jesus Christ. He was there, as real and substantial as the hum of the respirator.

While there were scattered moments of peace, frequent times of disorientation darken my days. I would lay there in the Intensive Care Unit, with so many unanswered questions, searching for explanation. Daily frustration came from lack of comfort created by the pumps, IV, catheter, pins, and rods that sustained every function of my small body. Loneliness came from the inability to communicate, thrusting me far into the depths of depression. Naturally, I felt separated from the world. There was no more amusement in my life. No more childish play. My innocence was replaced with survival, endurance, and a diminutive existence.

The days in the hospital seemed infinite. My father's visits were the only thing I had to anticipate. He would arrive every other day. Early in the mornings he would arrive with a handheld tape recorder. It would have a message from my momma that he recorded the day before. She would tell me that she loved me, missed me, and to get well soon. It was so uplifting. It helped bridge the separation between us. Her voice provided me with thoughts of contentment and affection. I missed her terribly. I would close my eyes and imagine the day when I could be in her arms again.

My visits with my father often included stories and music. He always found an opportunity to sing my favorite song, *I Love you a Bushel and a Peck*. He was slightly off-key and made up most of the words, but it still brought a smile to my face. He would wet a washcloth, then spin it around and around, and place it on my forehead. It was a welcomed relief from the extreme hot flashes that radiated through my body. My spinal cord injury had affected my body's ability to acclimate temperature. No longer able to sweat, I found the *cold rag* to be my only source of cooling refreshment.

He would tell me about the weather outside my hospital window and paint visual pictures with his words. It was the only glimpse I had of the world beyond the walls of my hospital room. When the nurses would come in to administer medication, my father would insist that they bring an extra syringe. He had brought from home my favorite doll, Victoria. The nurses would pretend to give the doll a shot with the empty syringe, and then apply a pediatric bandage to her arm. It was their attempt to divert my attention from the daily regimen of medicines.

The mind-altering, pain-relieving narcotics were the worst. I hated the feeling! The pain would still be there, just in a slightly different way. The drugs would induce sleep and cause incontrollable itching. Feelings of irritability emerged as tremors, and severe vomiting became a normal occurrence. My heart rate and blood pressure were elevated along with excessive chills alternating with flushing. The medicines also altered my thoughts. I had terrifying nightmares. I would often awake sobbing for my parents. The only thing that seemed real was the loneliness.

On my good days, when my father was there, I came to recognize his difficulty in leaving. As the sun began to set and the shadows spilled into my hospital room, I knew the time had come for my father to leave and return home. As bad as I wanted him to stay, I would close my eyes and pretend to be asleep. Soon after, I would hear him rise from his chair and leave the room. I would then open my eyes and feel the immeasurable sadness once again. I would cry. I would pray. And I found peace only in my sleep. Only in my dreams I would once again walk, run, peddle a bike, jump rope, dance, and twist with ease. Each day waking to my reality, I battled the truth of it all, over and over.

The feeding tube down my throat was my source of nourishment, the respirator was my source of breath, and the taped messages from my mother were my source of motivation. Instinctively, I knew nothing would ever be the same.

I hear someone screaming. Am I dreaming? I have to wake up. I have to open my eyes. It's hard to wake up. My eyes — they're heavy, they won't open. My head, it's foggy. I feel something heavy. I can hear someone, far away in a tunnel, screaming! She seems scared. Why is she crying? Where am I? I'm lost. Pain, oh, the pain. I'm tied up! Trapped in a cage. My legs are caught, stuck in a hole. I have to be dreaming. The voice; the screaming! I know that voice. I have to open my eyes. Why won't they open? I want to help, but I'm tied up. Why am I tied up? Somebody, anybody, let me out of this cage! I have to help. I must help. Let me out of this cage!

In the blink of an eye, it happened. My family trapped in scattered wreckage. Motionless, my grandmother lay there with me in her arms. My mother was pinned between the automobile steering wheel and driver's door, and my sister, alert and stunned by the sheer fear of what she saw. My sister, with her head in her hands, pleaded, ***"Oh God, please help us!"***

It was a tractor trailer, a sixteen wheeler, carrying tons of long pulp wood. My mother saw the truck in her lane. Captained by a drunk driver it was plowing straight for our car. Smoked filled the air from the tires, as the truck driver forced the brakes, but it was too late. My mother reacted quickly. She steered the car off the road and avoided a head-on collision. My mother fought hard to regain control of the automobile, returning back to the asphalt, and crossing the center line. We came to a sudden stop when an oncoming van crashed into the passenger side of our car. I was in my grandmother's lap. With her arms wrapped tightly around me, she slouched there, breathless. It was as though she had absorbed the impact to spare my life. And on August 17, 1979, on a country desolated road, I was plucked from my grandmother's final protective embrace. In scattered shards of glass lie a family who exists amongst death and disaster. Moments before, it had been an average day. The mundane had become critical and time was stained with uncertainty. In those four seconds when our car was totally out of control, my life changed. My family as I had known it was no longer.

What was to become of the ruins?

I was fashioned by twisted metal and glass shards on the wrong side of a two lane country road. I was given a second chance to rise again, as a broken youngster, from the hot asphalt pavement. Forthcoming I would be offered the opportunity to claim the driver's seat to a special destiny.

"Conquerors are not born; they are made, and the recipe is often quite egregious. Champion's are fashioned from adversity; forcefully carved from obstacles too monstrous to conceive. Yet somehow they survive and will themselves forward."

–Pam Baker

Dependence Came Ushering In

Though a righteous man falls seven times, he rises again.
–Proverbs 24:16

I can only imagine those first days of my injury and the first words that the physicians spoke to my father. What emotions did he experience? Or perhaps, was he even capable of feeling the pain? Paralyzed by his own fear and incapable of processing the magnitude of loss, what flooded his mind?

"How will I tell my child the problems she will now have to encounter? How do I explain urine backing up into her kidneys? How can a four-year-old understand urinary retention? What about the skin breakdown, and bedsores, and the constant infections, which can come anytime, and whose symptoms she won't even recognize. How do I tell my child she will never be able to have her own family?"

What about my mother? She lay there in a hospital bed of her own, with life-threatening injuries calculating in her mind. *"I am thirty-two years old. When Leslie is forty, I will be sixty-eight years old. I don't know how long or if I will be able to handle Leslie at home. I'm injured myself. Oh, how will I care for my child?"*

I'm sure there were people to help my parents with all the details. But the rehab hospital was not always going to be at their disposal. And the support of their friends would soon come to an end. The time would occur when my care was dependent upon my family. The staff at the rehab was clear that the requirements for a healthy quality of life would be demanding.

There was a conversation where physicians suggested that I would have to go somewhere — assisted care, a nursing home — a facility that had skilled staff to deal with the grueling challenges of my injury. They strongly urged my parents to consider the stresses that my care would bring to their life if they choose to care for me on their own.

The physicians were essentially illustrating their expectations, which must have seemed to my parents as permanent imprisonment for their child. By the time other kids in my generation would be having careers, families and establishing homes of their own, I would be sent to be cared for by strangers. The repeated question of "the quality of life" preoccupied every decision my parents had to make. The effect of my spinal cord injury traumatized my entire family. The anguish and feelings of anger, sadness, and guilt that came to my family — father, mother, and sister — is beyond what I could ever envision.

Trust is defined as *reliance or confidence in ability*. The dictionary first recognizes it as a noun. But if trust is viewed as a verb, the definition is: *to believe that someone is honest and will not harm you.* Trust is something that we talk about. We trust our family, we trust our friends. We say we trust God. But trust is a tricky thing. It is natural to question, *How can we believe in somebody? When can we be sure?* But trust is made **real** when we are forced to put it into action.

That is exactly what my injury has required me to do. I have been forced to put trust into action. You see, faith and trust are similar. For example, **Faith** indicates persistent action, devotion, and direction of self while **Trust** indicates a depth and a sense of assurance. Both are experienced only when they are in action. If I were able to walk, there would be many circumstances I would be able to control. But after paralysis, I had to learn to accept the things that I was incapable of doing independently. Because I can no longer rely on my legs, I have learned that I must put my trust in others.

Now, there are still those times when I have my doubts. When my trust is put to test, I question, *How and when can I believe in somebody? When can I be sure?*

Like the time my father first picked me up: getting out of the bed was something I could no longer do independently, therefore I had to *trust* that my father was capable of doing this for me. I had to have *faith* that I would not fall.

I will never forget the first time my father picked me up. It was the first day I moved from the hospital bed, with the cast on my leg, and with IVs, tubes, ventilator, and catheter, still connected. My father said, "Now Sweetheart, just relax. I'm going to put my arm under your legs and one arm around your waist. Then I'm going to lift you up, out of the bed." I was so excited. This would be the first time I had been picked up since my injury. Then he did it, just as he told me. *It was awful!* I wanted to tell him that I was afraid; it felt as if he would drop me. I could not feel his arms under me or around me. My legs dangled, feeling heavy, like stone cold rocks. My arms were too weak to place around him for more security. He whispered, "Trust me." I saw the love in his face. He sat there for hours, with me in his arms. Because of the ventilator, I was unable to speak; I couldn't tell him that I was frightened. Even though I couldn't feel his touch, I found security in being close. He was the only thing that made sense in my life right now, the only constant. He became my source of wisdom, my comforter, my rescuer. And even though he had amazing strength, nothing prepared him for this moment. He sobbed uncontrollably. I can only imagine the prayers that he must have prayed. "*Oh Lord, take this from my child and make it my burden. Take my legs, not hers. Make it my pain.*" I think that's exactly what my father set out to do. From that moment on, my father embraced my injury and made it his mission to discover every possible option available to improve the quality of my life.

Each day there was a new set of obstacles with different solutions. As I continued to fight for my life, my mother was in her own battle of survival. She was praying for stability. She had multiple bone injuries that needed immediate surgery, but she would have to wait until the internal bleeding could be controlled. Three times surgeons prepared her body for surgery, and within minutes of anesthesia, her cardiovascular system failed. Three times physicians were certain they had lost her. But, to their amazement and without medical explanation, they watched my mother recover from her injuries.

Multiple surgeries mended and repaired her crushed hip and femur. God guided the skilled hands of numerous orthopedic surgeons. Certainly, God was not finished. My mother had a divine purpose and a reason to survive.

My father became artful at a delicate balancing act. His time was spent equally between the two hospitals. I was in a children's hospital, in Birmingham, Alabama, and my mother was in a hospital in Opelika, Alabama, which required my father to travel more than seventy miles a day. The damage to my spine exposed my emotions in an amplified way. My family not only had to deal with my fear, confusion, anxiety, and despair, but also their own misery. The closeness I had once known in my family became stretched so far that the cracks slowly began to show. The crushed vertebra seemed to be the beginning of a fracture, iny my family, one that eventually destroyed the relationships I so deeply loved. There were the medical bills and my sister, who need my parents more than ever. Our future was dim and dull. I am certain that the only way we survived as a family was through Christ Jesus. I sensed His presence. Surely my family sensed Him too.

Instinctively, my mother's only choice was to absorb the entire responsibility of caring for me. Together, my mother and father made the decision that he would continue his role of financially supporting the family. The extensive medical, equipment, and therapy bills were escalating and would require many overtime hours, but somehow we would make it. I will be forever grateful for the unselfish decision my parents made. But, in the midst of the relentless feeling of mere survival, I concluded that I was to blame for the slow unraveling of my family. I began to recognize a shift in our family dynamics and held myself responsible for the added stress.

Under the pressure of loss, each of my family members was given a chance to refine their faith. Would we falter or persevere? Would we accept it with gratitude or grief? It would only be in gratitude and acceptance that we would find grace, which we needed to obey the Lord and overcome this tragedy. It would be in grief that my family would be tempted and derailed.

Conclusive statistics regarding the divorce rate of couples with disabled children are not available. There is a consensus that the rate is significantly higher, possibly elevated by 75%. Yet, it should be noted that there are many husbands and wives who report having strong marriages while raising children with disabilities. Supporting evidence certainly lies withing the families who choose to adopt children who are disabled.

Faith Can Rewrite the Future

Though he brings grief, he will show compassion, so great in his unfailing love. For he does not bring affliction or grief to the children of men.
–Lamentations 3:32-33

Jesus is moved with compassion for those who are hurting. Any father would do everything in his power to help his suffering child. My father was no exception. He quickly took matters into his own hands and searched for ways to make my recovery easier. He knew that our life at home would never be the same. Our house did not provide enough space. The bathrooms were too small for the metal framed, 50-pound wheelchair — a primitive piece of equipment that posed more conflict than independence. It served its purpose, but was a far cry from the freedom of my wheelchair today.

After the initial learning and adjustment process had been accepted, my parents began to plan for my return home. In order for our home to be accessible, my father had to remodel. The living room was enlarged and modifications to the bathroom were made. A nurse was hired to help with the daily regimen.

I had to become stronger before physicians would discharge me. Breathing on my own, feeding myself, sitting upright for long periods of time; I had to regain an intermediate level of strength in order to return home. Day by day I improved, as my mother matched my progress.

In November, one week before Thanksgiving, I came home. I boarded a plane. Tom Houston's, a local candy factory distributor, donated the services of their private jet. Our neighbors, Dean and Betty Pickard, worked hard to make the arrangements. It was my first flight, a journey to independence. Like a butterfly fresh from its chrysalis, I was weak and fatigued. Yet, I was eager to prepare for my new life beyond the safe habitat I had known for more than twelve weeks. The flight took less than hour, and I found myself in a place that was familiar. For the first time, in my wheelchair, I returned to the only house I had ever known, and it was wonderfully safe.

The next day, my father and I made the trip to Opelika. My father pushed me in my wheelchair and then parked me outside of a hospital room door. "I'll be right back," he said. Within moments he returned. With a smile and tears in his eyes, he bent down to my level. He said, "Are you ready to see your mommy?" I don't think I said a thing. I just smiled.

There, in a hospital gown, in a room filled with flowers, was my mom. I saw her cry. For the first time, she saw me, her child, confined to a wheelchair. Nothing could have prepared her. Beneath the tears was a smile. She reached for my hand. She gathered her thoughts. "Oh, Leslie, I'm so glad to see you," she pulled me close. Unable to stifle my emotions, I cried. She was like a beacon of light. She was a source of hope, and I knew my journey to regain the life I had once known had just begun.

A week later my mom returned home. The home health care nurse was setting up our necessary items: a bed pan, lotions, ointments, and medicines. Our bedrooms had been transformed. As the nurse explained where she had placed everything. A thought pierced my mind: *Where is my grandmother?* I was never told that my grandmother would be at this reunion; I just assumed that she would.

I struggled to find any reasonable reason why she wasn't here. "Dad! Dad!" I shouted, attempting to divert his attention to me. "Wait a minute," he replied, as he attended to my mothers needs. Impatiently I demanded, "Dad, where is Muner?" Muner was the name of affection we called my grandmother. "Why is she not here?" The nurse looked at me then toward my father. He then looked at my mother. It was in that moment that I sensed something was wrong. I had replayed in my mind over and over what it would feel like to reunite with my grandmother. And with one question came the answer that no child deserves to hear. My Muner had died. She had taken her last breath the day of the accident. My father picked me up and placed me in the bed along side my mother. She held me there for hours, until eventually I cried myself to sleep.

I had not been told of her death while I was in the hospital because the physician thought it was best to protect me from unnecessary emotional stress. Any additional pain could have slowed my progress. My parents' explanation was delivered in a delicate way, yet the pain and emptiness was still there. I knew my grandmother was in heaven, but I wanted her here with me. In the weeks ahead, my mother and father would comfort me with stories of how much Muner loved me. In time, they answered all my questions.

Although I was young, I came to recognize that Muner was still with me. I realized the bond we held defied the fatal weight of finalization. Her faith in Jesus Christ as her personal Savior made me certain that our relationship was intact. My friendship and love with her did not end; it just took on a more intimate form. This truth would be reconfirmed throughout my life, much like the day Dylan was born. The nurse named Dot was enough confirmation for me that she had been appointed my guardian angel the day she left earth and stepped into heaven. The sweetest reminders of Muner have occurred in my times of weakness.

So often we look for miracles presented perfectly, ready for a majestic appearance. We search for miracles that enter our lives with trumpets and brass horns. In truth, God responds to us in whispers and through the sweep of angels' wings. They are among us, giving us gifts that quietly offer God's grace and protection. For me, I have faith that Muner still walks with me, bringing gifts of blessings.

After Christmas, my mother and I were both showing signs of improvement. The return to our own environment had heightened our desire to reclaim our lives. But it still was difficult. There were many afternoons that my mother and I spent together. Sometimes she would cry. I wondered if she was missing her mother. Maybe she was crying for me, or because of her pain. I understand now that she was probably crying about it all.

On her good days she would play with me. My favorite game was "doctor and patient", a theatrical role-playing pastime where my mother was the patient and I was the doctor. I would take a tongue depressor and methodically place it on my mother's back. I would apply pressure and say, "Can you feel that?" It was something I had become accustomed to; the doctors had used a similar method in rehab. Instead of a tongue depressor they

Mom and me after our recovery.

would use a pin, poking and probing different parts of my body. This examination was used to help determine my level of sensation. It was something I hated. The thought of a sharp pin being placed in areas of my body that I could no longer feel was agonizing. But, now that I was home, I found it entertaining to put my mother through the same rigorous test. Looking back, I can't help but laugh. It would always surprise me when my mother could feel below my level of sensation. In my young mind, my mother's injuries should have mirrored mine. Although she could walk, I had convinced myself that since she was in the same accident, the same loss of sensation applied to her. To humor me, she would sometimes say that she couldn't feel. Silly, I know, but it made me feel like I was not alone.

Oreo, my toy poodle, was also a unique friend who offered me companionship through my recovery. She had been my first pet and a dear friend since the day I brought her home. Her dedication to me was unconditional. Before my paralysis, our favorite pastime together was swinging on the backyard swing. On late summer afternoons, Oreo and I would pretend that she was a guest at my private tea party. Dressed in a pink lacey dress and bonnet, with black and white puppy fur spilling out over her ears, she could have passed for Laura Ingall's twin sister. Patiently, Oreo would sit there, watching me pour tea into plastic cups. She would lap up the sweet refreshment and wait for her next serving.

While I was in the hospital, my father told me that Oreo was missing our time together. In fact, my kind, gentle companion had become a growling giant who would aggressively chase anyone away from our swing set — anyone who dared to come within a few feet of it. She ate very little. My father explained that she was grieving. When I first returned home it was gratifying to me that Oreo recognized me instantly. She jumped into my lap, tail wagging, with an endless supply of wet "doggy sugar." She was nonjudgmental. It didn't take long for Oreo and me to rediscover the things we loved. My father would pick me up and placed me on the swing, and once again we enjoyed our afternoon teas.

As I embraced my changed life, so did my dog. Her friendship held true to *woman's best friend*. Ironically, two years after my paralysis, Oreo woke one morning unable to walk. We rushed her to the veterinarian. X-rays revealed that Oreo had damaged a vertebra in her spine. The veterinarian informed us that our only option was to euthanize. I cried and begged for another solution. I could live with paralysis, so why couldn't my dog? The vet described the great pain she would endure and her inability to lead a healthy life. At the time, she was already nine years old. The vet continued to explain that that was considered to be a normal life expectancy for a dog. My pain was no less and my desire to hold on to my beloved pet

My pet, Oreo. Together we enjoyed a Honda 70 three-wheeler. This ATV allowed me to experience a sense of freedom from my wheelchair.

overshadowed all reasonable explanations. Hadn't I been through enough? Why were the most precious things being stripped from my life?

I sat with Oreo as she took her last breath. I whispered in her ear, "Thank you for being a faithful friend. You were a good dog." She slowly drifted off to sleep.

I believe dogs go to heaven. Christ had given me great joy in the companionship of my pet. How could they not have a resounding place of eternal bliss? Although I was young, I was beginning to understand that loss was a natural part of life. In the grips of grief, once again, I could sense the unfailing love of Jesus. I was learning that often God's gifts seem unwanted. I began to see that life may take things away, but life also gives back. And endowment can often be discovered in ways that we least expect.

Reclaiming My Life

I guide you in the way of wisdom and lead you along straight paths.
When you walk, your steps will not be hampered; when you run you will
not stumble.
–Proverbs 4:11-12

I came to realize that I would spend the rest of my life responding to questions. I would have questions of my own and then there were always the inquiries of others. It wasn't long before I noticed a reoccurring query people would ask, *"Leslie how come you have such a positive attitude?"*

That was the easy part for me. My mind-set was the one variable that I was still capable of controlling. My legs no longer responded to my commands. My hands were too weak to comb my hair. But my approach on life was under my control. And I planed to use my intelligence to shape an affirmative lifestyle.

You see, God did not turn His back on me. That hot summer day, when time seemed to stand still, when the humid air seemed stole every last breath of hope, God was there. Like a cool drink of water replenishing a thirsty soul, God filled me up with sanguinity. I understood the importance of my perseverance. I saw the value in having a positive attitude.

When you're disabled, you have limitations that are easily noticed, and then there are the things that are hidden. With a spinal cord injury, the loss of function and the inability to walk are noticed. Often the paralysis in my legs is the part of my disability people understand. In fact, they believe that this is the only problem I have sustained. In my opinion, not being able to walk is slightly more than an inconvenience. It's the things that come with paralysis that demean and degrade.

To begin with, you must understand the complexity of SCI (*spinal cord injury*). I am considered a quadriplegic. The level at which my spinal cord was either severed or bruised is the seventh cervical vertebra. In medical terminology, I am referred to as a *C-7 quadriplegic, incomplete*. The "incomplete" gives the indication that there is not a complete injury in the spinal cord — an assumption that my spinal cord was damaged, but not severed. Bruising could have occurred. If the spinal cord swells, permanent nerve damage is certain. The exact condition of my injured spinal cord is unknown because of the inability to conclude without exploratory surgery. To have surgery for the sake of a conclusive diagnosis is something I have rejected. Although every SCI is unique in itself, there are a few determining factors for a complete or incomplete injury. My mobility resembles the function of an incomplete injury, which ultimately means that my mobility is better than if I were considered to have sustained a complete injury.

Paralyzed legs are one of the effects of SCI. Quadriplegics, however, suffer many more conditions than paralysis in the lower extremities. *Quad*, meaning four, refers to all limbs having limited mobility. My legs, arms, and hands all have some level of paralysis. For example, my right arm is more affected than my left. The grip in my right hand produces less than one pound of pressure, while my left hand can provide a stronger grip. This has required me to relearn many daily activities using only my left hand. Holding a pencil, using utensils, combing my hair, and tying my shoes were all tasks I had to relearn. The lack of muscle control in both of my hands has made the tendons and ligaments degenerate (shrinking or become smaller, weakening and reducing my ability). The appearance of my hands is drawn and aged.

When I was five, only eleven months after my injury, my physician referred me to a neurologist. He would measure my progress and offer suggestions for further therapy. My parents hoped that we could find ways to improve my hand strength and find bracing or equipment that might assist in daily activities. Anything that could help me in becoming more independent was always a need in my life. Once we were in the specialist's office, my parents explained the history of my injury. My parents entered this opportunity with anticipation and excitement in learning more. The doctor proceeded to ask questions. My mother provided any information that would help him make proper suggestions. The specialist said very little. He was indirect and said nothing to me prior the examination. The doctor took my right hand. One by one, he moved my fingers, rotated my wrist, and asked me to grip his hand as hard as I could. With a smile, I looked at him and said, "That's all I've got." My fingers slightly touched his. A duck with webbed feet had a better grip than I. He held my hand up in the air, pulling my arm closer to my parents. He said, "This is what we call a *claw hand*." And with that one statement, my father looked the physician in the eyes and demanded to see him in the hallway. Once outside, my father reminded him that he was dealing with a five-year-old child, newly injured. He drew closer to the doctor in the white lab coat and politely, yet forcefully, said, "Don't ever refer to a child's hand as a 'claw hand.' I suggest you change the way you deal with children. Whether my daughter's hand can grip or not, it's precious to me. Your terminology stinks, and you can take you specialist degree and hang it in your bathroom. As far as I'm concerned, you need higher education in the human emotions." And with that we left. My father taught me more than I could have ever learned from the neurologist. His passion about how I was perceived, as well as how I perceived myself, would be a powerful foundation that I built my life upon.

My hands may not work the way they were designed to, but I can effectively use them in most tasks. Nerve damage in the spinal cord also affects sensation. For instance, the top side of my arm has full sensation, yet on the underside of my arm I can feel only pressure. Hot, cold, rough, and soft are all sensations that I can no longer feel on the under sides of my arms. This can be dangerous.

One morning, when I was in middle school, I was getting ready for school. As usual, I woke early so I would have plenty of time to primp and make myself into a fashionable, trendy teen. At this age, I could be very fussy about my appearance. On this particular morning, I was having a bad hair day. I curled my hair over and over. Trying my best to tame my frizzy hair, I rushed as I was already late. I smelled something burning. I went on thinking my mother had over-cooked my breakfast. Suddenly, I realized that my arm was on top of my hot curling iron. I quickly withdrew my arm and looked at the torched underside of my wrist. My bad hair day was now the least of my problems. My mother rushed me to the ER. I was informed that I had incurred third degree burns. That would require weeks of treatment.

The pain from the burn eventually emerged. Although I could not feel topical pain the burn had penetrated deeper tissue permitting awareness of the injury. My emotions over came me. I looked at my mom. "Momma, why do I have to go through so much?" She placed her hand on top of mine in a devoted affection way. A touch only a mother could provide and said, "Leslie, you're strong. God knows that. You've been through much worse."

As the physician bandaged my arm, I quietly cried. I thought of the many people I had seen at clinics and hospitals that did not have their arms. The people that were in sip and blow wheelchairs, those who were paralyzed from their neck down. I was in pain but I knew those people would welcome this experience; that the ache of the scorch would be a blessing to those who had lost sensation of their arms. I suppressed my emotions and became thankful for the pain I was allowed to experience.

After an assortment of ointments and barrier wraps, my arm healed. I learned many valuable lessons, from the gratitude of having the ability in my arms to paying attention. I gained the knowledge to be mindful of those less fortunate.

Worship Jesus today, in this very moment. Give your thanks to Him alone for everything you have, *even if you don't have all you want.* Give humble gratitude to Him for the things you have and the blessings in your life, for there are others who have so much less.

Motor skills, like walking, hand grip, and finger dexterity, are functions I obviously desire to have back. But the one thing that is mortifying is the loss of bladder function. To be incontinent, unable to control the muscles of the bladder, is degrading, to say the least. This is a very difficult subject to discuss. Since I was injured at such a young age, I could not fully grasp what it meant to be incontinent. I chose to hide this part of my life in fear that others would not understand.

Intermittent catheterization was adapted in the early eighties as the method of bladder management for SCI. Today it is used widely and helps those of us with SCI lead a healthy and independent life. Although it is necessary, I have been able to hide this aspect for most of my life. It wasn't until I was in college that I fully accepted what must be done. For years, I had battled depression and shame because it was difficult to deal with the circumstance. It is also the one obstacle that hinders me more than my mobility. It is time-consuming, it exposes me to health risks, and it's inconvenient. Nevertheless, it is necessary. Catheterization, and the fear of people not understanding, has been a source of insecurity. I still struggle with this, but I do my best and understand that it's something I cannot change. Like the Serenity Prayer says,

God grant me the serenity to accept the things I cannot change; courage to change the things I can; and wisdom to know the difference.

There were many times I would remind myself of this prayer. And still there were those time that I thought my disability was going to defeat me.

Entering middle school and becoming a teenager brings a whole batch of pressures. Being a middle schooler in a wheelchair possess its own set of difficulties. This stage of my life was marked by recognizing the differences in my life. My inability to care for my basic needs became a source of insecurity. School was no longer a place of enjoyment and learning but more of a taunting place of my inadequacies. I searched for ways to fit in. I was determined to not become known as *"the girl in the wheelchair"*. It was almost as though I was compelled to over compensate for my lack of independence. I was in a constant search for acceptance -developing the need for popularity.

In the first days of my middle school, I heard my peers talking about the upcoming tryouts for the cheerleading team. I began to envision the recognition that would come with making the squad. Certainly if I could accomplish cheerleader status I would be accepted.

At first mention of my plans to my mother I was meet with opposition. Out of her concern and wiliness to protect me from failure she sweetly tried to direct my attention to a more attainable goal. "Leslie, I know that there is a position for cheerleader manager. The team needs an organized leader that can keep up with equipment inventory, manage a calendar, and orchestrate community involvement. You would be a great manager," my momma encouraged. But my determination had already set in and I ambitiously set out to make the team. I began to devise a comprehensive plan for tackling the tryouts. Initially I visited with the coach and discussed the requirements and informed her that I would be trying out for the team. Once again I was offered the position of management and once more I declined. By now I had learned the value in challenging others.

When anyone would tell me that *I could not* or *should not* do something it was like adding fuel to an already lit fire. Their doubts propelled my determination.

I emphasized to the coach the need to be judge on the same standards as others. Then I solicited the help from former cheerleaders. Hours of practice, preparation, and developing the best use of my arm mobility consumed all my free time for the next few weeks.

When the day arrived to demonstrate my ability, I wheeled out onto the auditorium stage, which at the time seemed enormous, flaunted a superlative smile, and gave it my best shot. I projected my voice and precisely moved my arms sharply. With a voice of a giant I chanted:

Ram fans in the stands yell Orange and Green,
-Then I clapped.-
Yell Orange and Green.
-Then I popped a wheelie-
Come on fans get up off your feet and listen to the Rams beat go

And in a rhythmic mix of claps and wheelies, I stirred excitement among the judges and teachers that looked on.
We say Orange, You say Green. Orange…green…orange green.
Go Rams!

I knew that becoming a cheerleader would require commitment. Academic, physical, behavioral expectations were all components of becoming a part of the schools cheer squad. These were the least of my concerns. By far they were attainable. But after my performance during tryouts I worried about how my peers would react. Would they think I was looking for a pity vote? If I made the team would my peers ever recognize that I was chosen based on merit? Or would I always have to fight to prove myself worthy of the uniform?

Then if I didn't make the team-which was more likely-would I have to face the whispers of pity and sorrow that I was just *"the girl in the wheelchair"* who unfortunately could not acquire her dream. What ever the case I knew there would certainly be forthcoming challenges.

The results were posted the next day. It was a Saturday and my mom drove me to the school gymnasium. I saw the uncertainty in her face.

I thought she must be carefully planning the delicate words of encouragement needed to soften the blow when my name was not on the list. However, she never needed to use those painstaking words. Instead there were words of congratulations. In amazement there located on a list, among eleven other names, was my name. It was official. I was an Arnold Middle School Cheerleader. I couldn't help but think about my sister. She was a cheerleader at the time of the accident. Was it part of my destiny to walk in her footsteps?

The Ram cheerleaders help lead the football team to state conference that year. It turned out, that cheerleading was so much more than a quest for popularity. It was an opportunity for me to become an ambassador for my school and community. I was given the chance to develop teamwork, personal responsibility and integrity. My personal perseverance to not be defined by my limits was a foundation to the success I found in the sport of cheerleading. It was where I develop the personal motto to *live not by circumstance but according to where I wanted to go*.

My school year ended and my teammates made plans to go to cheer camp during the summer. Me, however, I had to go to independent living camp. Shepherd Spinal Center in Atlanta, Georgia was a specialty hospital that offered post injured patients independent living skills. I would be admitted to the hospital as an inpatient and my duration would be for three weeks. I entered into this situation with enthusiasm as my parents had described compared this experience to "going off to college and having my own dorm room." My thoughts of hall parties and summer flings were quickly dispelled.

This is where I would first learn about autonomic dysreflexia. Autonomic dysreflexia (AD) , also known as hyperreflexia, is a state that is unique to patients after spinal cord injury. Autonomic dysreflexia can develop suddenly, and is a possible emergency situation. If not treated promptly and correctly, it may lead to seizures, stroke, and even death. The seriousness of this condition gave rationalization for inducement of symptoms.

After two days at Shepherd Spinal Center, with out my knowledge, the physician allowed medications to produce hyperflexia. I was not made aware of the onset of the symptoms because it was imperative for me to come to recognize the symptom. Having the ability to quickly spot autonomic dysreflexia indicators could prove to be a life saving technique.

There I was eating my lunch-*which I remember tasting like typical hospital food*-and the room began to spin. Dizziness, a pounding headache, *which was caused by the elevation in my blood pressure*, goose pimples, sweating, and red blotching of my skin quickly emerged. I was scared and struggled to kept my head upright. The nurses, who had been aware that my symptoms would be brought on very quickly, came to my rescue. Within moments I was out cold. I'm sure a couple of hours slipped away before I was alert and aware of the entire situation. There can be many stimuli that cause AD. Anything that might have been painful, uncomfortable or physically irritating before the injury, such as broken bone, pressure sore, wounds or possibly bladder stones may cause autonomic dysreflexia after the injury. Once I fully recovered from this frightening and painful ordeal I was educated about how to avoid the life threatening disorder of AD. I learned how I could safe guard myself and what medications were available to help should I ever experience the symptoms again.

My stay at Shepherd Spinal Center, although necessary, was a far cry from what I had visualized. I would sit in my hospital room and wonder what my fellow teammates were doing at the exact time.

Trust in the Lord with all your heart and lean not on your own understanding; in all you're your ways acknowledge him, and he will direct your paths.
-Proverbs 3, 5-8

Even though it is common for parents to have difficulty letting go of their children as they mature, this transition can be even more challenging when the child has a disability. This was the case for me. At school age, I was developing my sense of identity and began to feel anxious or frightened as a result of my physical limitations. I despised the lack of control over my own environment. I detested the fact that I had to depend on so many people, parents, peers, and teachers to assist me in, essentially, every task in my life. Paralysis took away my independence.

Things you now take for granted, take more of my efforts or require complete assistance from others. For example, dressing is a task of physical exertion. Approximately, forty-five minutes of my morning is devoted to dressing. And if there are buttons involved, add another fifteen minutes to this regimen. But, in my moments of lost independence, I discovered a deepened dependence upon God. Reliance came ushering in. I have come to realize that it is, in fact, one of the greatest blessings that came from losing my legs: the intensified awareness of trust on Jesus Christ.

I understand that not everyone can connect or identify with my injury. But I do know that we are linked by the common thread of loss. Bereavement is something that affects us all and requires multiple levels of processing. Everyone has the choice to react and rightfully respond in their own way. It is only natural that there are those days that I just can't find the motivation to smile and gracefully move forward. Yes, there are those days that I cry and grieve for the things I wish I could physically do. I question, *What is God's objective for my limited life?* The struggles can seem overwhelming when it's an uphill battle just to care for your self. To be a quadriplegic is not at all the design I had for my life. In spite of this, God uses me, just as I am. Even on those days I toil.

I still remember the days I spent in the hospital, like a recorded movie. The desperation and helplessness on occasion withdraws me out from melancholy. Although I wish that I could record over these terrible memories, it helps to remember just how far I have come.

Learning how to adapt has become my decree. The single best equipment for me to succeed is prayer. To be connected in an intimate relationship with Jesus allows me to not stay in that place of mourning the loss but to learn how to acknowledge the things I do have.

In the Pursuit of Success

As each one has received a special gift, employ it in serving one another,
as good stewards of the manifold grace of God.
−1 Peter 4:10

Are you waiting for the perfect situation to come in order to find success in your life? Have you allowed excuses to hinder your achievements? If you can find success in the hardships of life you can make it work in all circumstance. You have to want success, you have to envision yourself succeeding, and you have to search for those opportunities that will help you reach your personal happiness.

Maneuvering in a wheelchair presents challenges. The occasional curb cut and electronic doors do help, but overall there will always be architectural barriers. It's just part of my life. It's not the world's responsibility to adapt to me but my duty to adapt to my surroundings.

Although I may be limited in my mobility I have the desire to strive for success in the professional world. When the time arrived, I wasted no time searching for a job. Well into my search for the perfect job, a wonderful opportunity presented itself. My friend, Ginger offered me a position as desk attendant at the Georgia Department of Trade and Tourism. My duties would require me to greet tourists visiting the state, offer advice to the best attractions, and assist in directions. Georgia is such a wonderful state that offers bountiful scenery and unforgettable Southern charm. My hometown of Columbus, Georgia, was equally blessed with beauty and rich history. I accepted Ginger's offer and became an employee of the Georgia Welcome Center. This was a new start for fulfillment in my life as well as a new beginning to a friendship that would last a lifetime.

My first two weeks were spent learning about the local attractions Columbus was host to. The Bradley Theatre, located in Historic Uptown Columbus Landmark District, was opened to the public by Paramount Pictures in 1940. Named after the founder of the Columbus-based W.C. Bradley Company, the theatre was designed in the Golden Age of motion pictures. Decorated in neoclassical and art deco architecture, it posses one of the most impressive stages and proscenium arches in the country. Today, the theatre hosts concerts, corporate functions, and special events.

I became very familiar with Callaway Gardens. Over half of our visitors inquired about the Gardens. I would have to explain the 14,000-acre resort in great detail: "Callaway Gardens is a must-see," I would say, "Beautifully landscaped grounds include lakes, nature trails, and bike paths. Located in the Gardens are three golf courses, tennis courts, a sandy beach, and Sibley Horticulture Center." This, of course, was my favorite attraction. "The Sibley Horticulture Center is the home of a five-acre greenhouse with exotic and native plants. And, just steps away, is the Cecil B. Day Butterfly Center, a glass-enclosed butterfly conservatory housing butterflies from three continents. Would you care for directions?" I would conclude. The guest would eagerly wait as I mapped out with my highlighter pen the exact route to take to the famous Gardens.

I became so skilled and knowledgeable about my hometown that I began to sound like an area attraction brochure. Located behind the information counter was a soda dispenser. Each guest received a free, refreshing Coca-Cola. It was my responsibility to serve the sodas to the customers. Within the first couple of days at work, I came to realize that the task was more difficult than originally expected. The dispenser had a handle that was mounted about an inch too high. I had to stretch and over-extend my arm to control the handle. Once the flow of Coca-Cola started, it was strenuous to get the handle back up. I don't think I would be exaggerating if I said that I spilled nearly a gallon of soda within the first week of my first job. It became a sticky mess, literally. My father witnessed the intense effort I had to go through in order to deliver the sweet carbonated drink. He devised a solution that made my duty trouble-free. He took a sturdy rope and wrapped it around the dispenser handle. At the end of the rope dangled a small leather loop that allowed me to tug with little effort. Now the only sticky mess I had to worry about was the visitors harassing me for refills.

Monday through Friday I would report to the Welcome Center directly from high school. I continued to build my knowledge on the state's history and attractions. It was behind that information desk that I learned many valuable lessons. I developed a work ethic, dedication, and responsibility. I learned how to interact with the public and discovered that knowledge was priceless. The development of my mind and hunger for wisdom became an aspect in my life that would replace my physical ability. For instance, I learned that even in perfect situations, life can throw you into a "sticky mess." Quick thinking and insight recovered me from many delicate situations. I developed skills that I still use today. I took away a lot from this experience, but even more, I felt like I was part of a community. Southern born and southern bred, I was a part of Georgia, and Georgia was a part of me. My Southern roots became my treasured heritage.

Although I enjoyed my first job, there came a time when I wanted explore other professions. I would discover jobs ranging from retail sales to management, grocery clerk to bank teller, restaurant hostess to public relations director.

Each job offered me a new set of responsibilities with a new set of challenges. I can't help but laugh about one evening at closing, when I was a manager at Hickory Farms. A woman approached the register. As I rang up her order, my legs involuntary jumped — a muscle spasm. With that one sharp stir in my lower leg, my center of gravity was thrown off. Up in the air went the jar of mustard I was holding. I lay there on the floor in the middle of the store. The lady was terrified. I gathered my thoughts and asked the troubled customer for assistance. With a little instruction, she managed to get me upright. I reassured her that I was just fine. She then reached in her purse and said, "Young lady, give me five of those beef sticks and one of each of those dipping sauces." This more than doubled the size of her original order. I think her purchase was somewhat of a *pity procure*. I dared not try to talk her out of it after everything I had already put her through. At her age, I was just thankful I had not sent her into cardiac arrest. So, I totaled up her order, no questions asked.

As my passion for business grew, so did my desire to be independent. The next step in the process was to learn how to drive.

My mother hesitated when I told her that I wanted to get my driver's license. Like any other mother, I'm sure she dreaded the day that she would have to loosen the strings and let me experience a little more independence. I've come to realize that my mother had so much more to overcome than most mothers. I was asking her to let me get behind the wheel — presenting the opportunity for her to no longer be in control of the very thing that injured me. An automobile, in her mind, was the weapon of destruction and source of tragedy in our life.

Her hesitation and uncertainty gave way to reason and for the sake of moving forward. She agreed that driving would give me more independence, but of course, she insisted on a lengthy list of rules and regulations. We had a meeting of the minds, as I vowed to respect her rules. At the time, I had no clue the immense emotions and uncertainties she had to go through. I'm certain that she covered me with prayers of protection, praying for the maturity I needed to understand the responsibility of safe driving. But, like any other sixteen-year-old, I was on mission. To me, getting my driver's license was like a right of passage. Driving would be a source of release, freeing me from the confinement of my wheelchair, opening up a new world and space for me to explore.

It was early summer, just before my sophomore year in high school. My mother and father drove me to the nearby rehabilitation center, Roosevelt Warm Springs Institute for Rehabilitation. There I would learn how to drive with adaptive equipment. During the forty-five-minute drive, I envisioned how my day would be. In my mind's eye, I could see me behind the wheel of a sleek stylish new car with my driver instructor, a hunky handsome young therapist, and me, the perfect student, passing the driver's test on the first day. As we approached the campus of the rehabilitation center, sitting in the parking lot was an Oldsmobile that dated back to the sixties. Pale yellow with dents galore, the back bumper hanging on by only one screw, and swinging overhead was a mounted sign, lined with red blinking lights: "Student Driver." This had to be a joke. This is not the car I had dreamed of. The appearance alone was enough to make anyone second-guess getting a driver's permit. The size of the heavy bulky car would certainly prove to be a challenge. This car was unfashionable and undesirable, but I was teen that was eager for the liberty in driving.

The day began learning how to break down my wheelchair, first pulling off the wheels, placing them over in the passenger seat, then reclining the driver's seat, to ensure enough room for the frame of my chair to be safely pulled across my chest and placed in the passenger seat. I then had to reach over to buckle the equipment in place. It was, to say the least, tiresome and tedious. Three times I disassembled my chair, trying different angles and techniques.

The instructor showed me how the hand controls worked. "Push for brakes and pull for acceleration. Keep in mind that your movements need to be short and small because the hand controls are very sensitive. Are you ready to try?" he asked. I looked at the instructor and nodded. With what I thought was a small short pull, I revved up the engine as the RPMs jumped. "Oh my," the instructor said. "Dale Earnhart has a new contender." His sense of humor was welcome, but my expectations of being the perfect student had diminished with the first touch of the modified equipment.

Once I had adjusted to the sensitive hand controls, the instructor took a bold leap of faith. "Are you ready to go for a spin?" he asked. With a few gasps and jolts, I managed to maneuver the car onto the open road. It was a country road. Pastures and fences lined the road that meandered through the small town of Warm Springs, Georgia. About fifteen minutes into my first drive I approached a sharp curve. The instructor told me to slow my speed a little. As we were making our way around the curve, suddenly an object appeared. It was a cow! I swerved and instead of pushing forward for brakes, I panicked and pulled, accelerating towards the animal. The car spun into the dirt and the instructor grabbed the wheel and pushed the emergency brake that was on his side. We came to a screeching halt. I placed my head in my hands, slouched over the steering wheel, and cried. A bead of sweat rolled down the instructor's forehead. Other than that, he didn't appear to panic or show fear of what might have happened. He kept his composure and spoke calmly to me to make certain that I was okay.

He then laughed and said, "I must say that after twelve years of teaching Driver's Ed, this has been the most exciting ride yet." I politely smiled and glanced at the cow. The cow slowly meandered towards the other side of the road. He was oblivious to the event that had just taken place. The poor cow — he never knew that he almost became ground chuck that day.

I was stunned and too upset to drive any more that day. I transferred into the passenger seat, and the instructor drove us back to the rehab center. The ride back into Columbus was silent. My parents had learned of my close encounter from the instructor. Parental intuition made them realize that this subject was not open for discussion. They respected my willingness to try that day and simply told me, "Tomorrow will be a better day. It will take some time, but you will get the hang of it." I thought to myself, *tomorrow, not again tomorrow.* Exhausted and emotionally drained, I fell asleep in the backseat of our car, knowing that I had to try again. Somehow, I would learn to drive.

We traveled to driving school for more than three months. Twice a week I would go through the routine of breaking down my wheelchair and loading it behind the seat. Over and over I tested the hand controls before my voyage onto paved roads. With each trip, I regained confidence and saw improvement. It was hopeful and it was possible that I would get my license after all.

On September 10, 1990, my parents pulled up in the driveway in an equipped Buick Regal — burgundy, sleek, new, and mine. "Happy birthday," my father said. "Let's go get your driver's license." We drove downtown to the Motor Vehicle Department. I passed my drivers examination. My life was about to take on a new meaning.

Driving my car became my experience of newly-found freedom. I set out for the country roads, which I knew like the back of my hand by now, turned up the radio, and rolled down the windows. In that moment I felt like anyone else. It was empowering and encouraging. I loved the independence! Behind the steering wheel my wheelchair became non-existent.

I was so focused on my image and trying my best just to fit in. I vowed that I would always drive a small sporty car. There seemed to be this stereotype that as a disabled driver, one must drive a modified van. For years, I drove cars that reflected trend and style — from a Buick Regal to a Honda Civic, even upgrading to a dynamic high-performance Volvo. I loved that car. It was breathtaking!

But the day came when I recognized the value in finding ways to make my life easier. I considered a ramp van. Studying and researching what options exist, I found my choice of vehicles must no longer resemble those out-of-date, full conversion vans that I never wanted to drive. And, when I found the Independent Mobility Systems, Toyota Sienna wheelchair-accessible minivan, I was impressed with the style and look. Crossover vehicles and utility cars had become popular. The Toyota Sienna was in vogue and my choice of a modern ride that instantly made my life easier.

I think people understand that life can change in a matter of seconds. I also think that people think it will never happen to them. No one is immune to the occurrence of a spinal cord injury. Whether by automobile accident, gun shot, or misjudgment leading to a fall, people who sustain a spinal cord injury are forced to live life sitting down.

When first injured, one might reflect on, and desperately search for ways to a partial or complete cure. The desire for a total recovery can be consuming and become a daily focus. In the early stages of grieving, the loss of mobility can be devastating. However, there does come a time where one's focus shifts and life sitting down takes on a new purpose.

It might be hard for the newly injured to fathom the idea that one day their search for a cure will become a lower priority. And high level quadriplegics may have a longer period of adjustment. Don't misunderstand; the desire and the need for a cure will always be there. Like the steady beat of my heart, my desire to walk again is there — every day, every hour, every second. But the amount of time I allow myself to dwell and search has diminished as I have uncovered a quality of independent living. Now I spend my time enjoying each minute that God has granted me, for each day I have been given is a gift! Twenty-six years post-injury, I've learned that life is good. It doesn't matter if you are standing or sitting down. It's a matter of perspective.

Take a moment and ask yourself this question: How much time during the day do you sit down? At work, do you to sit at a computer? How about your daily commute? How long do you spend sitting in your car? Or air travel or sitting on a train? Whatever the case, I'm certain you spend a large amount of your day sitting down. My point: well, you and I are not much different. Outwardly, yes. Certainly I can't hide my ultra stylish wheelchair, nor do I wish to hide it. But, the mere fact that I look different does not support the assumption that I am different. On the other hand, I like being different.

God has equipped me with the strength to recognize that my disability is a gift. Sometimes the gifts we receive are not the gifts that we have asked for. And unlike a present that was purchased, my gift of disadvantage and loss is nonrefundable. But my gift does come with a warranty, *a promise*. God promised that He would not give us things we are incapable of handling. Not only does Christ empower me to successfully live my life with my disability, but He strengths me with the knowledge and desire to use my disability for His platform of greatness.

The Importance of Inner Beauty — but the outside matters too!

There are so many stereotypes that still exist for people in wheelchairs. In fact, it's hard to believe that there will one day be no stereotypes. They will always exist as long as there are opinionated people who refuse to see things from the perspective of others. The most common stereotype that I have faced is the notion that I should be bitter; that I should hang my head down low and settle for a meek, comfortable life that is safe within certain limits. Pushing the envelope, aspiring to blaze a new trail, are notions that should not reflect the life of a quadriplegic. Often times I am "pigeon-holed".

It's difficult for outsiders to understand that I am, in a sense, grateful for my injury. "Give thanks in all circumstances," the apostle Paul tells us. And this is how I feel in regard to my disability. One reason people struggle to understand how I can graciously accept my injury as a gift is that they retain resentment towards the complicated circumstances of their own lives. Financial difficulties, unruly children, and broken relationships can be hidden blessings, yet difficult to receive. Most people view such things as hardships and miss the significant opportunity each one possesses. It's more than finding the silver lining; it's about seeing the possibilities that are within every situation. It's how we choose to respond to each situation that determines the source of blessing we may or may not receive.

When the chips are down, always show your pizazz!

Facing stereotypes daily, I find it important to always take pride in my outward appearance. Inwardly I have accepted my differences and outwardly I must reflect this. I have to laugh, as I grasp what I must do every day, just to get to the place where I can think about outside beauty. After two hours of showering, catheterization, transfer to the bed, dress, and then transferring back into my wheelchair, I then can begin my makeup and beautifying process. And believe me, it's a process! Just like any other woman, it's important to me. I refuse to allow my woman-hood to be stripped away.

Often adults have questions they would like to ask, but out of respect, they don't ask. On the other hand, a child will be the first to ask, "Why are you in a wheelchair?" I feel that it is my duty to make the adults feel comfortable enough to ask me the same thing. I see it in their eyes; they all want to know. I have to understand that most people may not have had a direct experience with someone in a wheelchair. My acquaintance could possibly be their first. It is my responsibility to smile, to be friendly and well-spoken, even if someone has bad etiquette in asking inappropriate questions. The only way to educate people is to lead by example. That's why outward beauty matters, too. People instinctively look at me. The wheelchair makes it hard to blend in. So, if people are going to be watching, well, I want them to see a strong, secure woman.

Breaking Stereotypes

Appearance is just the beginning. We see all types of disabilities within our society: blindness, cerebral palsy, muscular dystrophy, and amputees, just to name a few. But how often do you see these populations reflected in mainstream media — movies, magazines, advertisements, and reality shows? Let's get real. The tapestry of America is a blend of differences. Our nation is made strong by individuality. Then, where is this reflected in our entertainment? Yes, there is the occasional role scripted for some-one using a cane or a wheelchair. The latest prime time role was on *CSI Miami*. Dr. Al Robbins, played by Robert David Hall, is an amputee. And then there was an episode where the disabled man was the villain. He escaped the crime scene but left his wheelchair behind. And future roles are in the works for the *CSI New York*, where writers have created a leading role for someone in a wheelchair. Hats off to CBS for breaking new ground in the entertainment industry.

But the scattered roles we occasionally see are a far stretch from appropriate representation for the 11,000 individuals who sustain a SCI each year and the 250,000 to 400,000 persons living with SCI (according to the National Spinal Cord Injury Association). And when has there ever been a role scripted for a woman in a wheelchair, who falls in love, and has a romantic encounter with a man? A love scene from a wheelchair? Yes it's possible. I should know. I have two children as souvenirs.

If mainstream media can realistically portray the lives of people with disabilities, stereotypes can be overcome.

A Sense of Humor

Dance as though no one is watching you.
Love as though you have never been hurt before.
Sing as though no one can hear you.
Live as though heaven is on earth.
— Souza

When you have to use a wheelchair for mobility, you might think that falling is no longer a problem. To the contrary, it happens more often than you can imagine. It's part of the territory. I have fallen down steps, fallen when my wheelchair comes to an abrupt stop, fallen in holes — I have fallen almost everywhere. Falling usually happens when I least expect it. Like the time I was out with my girlfriends. We were dancing at our favorite disco club. We were known for our weekend trips to the neighboring town of Auburn, Alabama. The lively southern campus was excitement and spirited. Auburn University was a short drive from my home. My girlfriends and I would save our small profits from our part-time jobs for gas money.

We would dance the night away. On this particular night, my favorite disco song, *I Will Survive* called for my presence on the dance floor. All the girls in the club danced impulsively, as if this song symbolized our freedom. We adopted this song as our anthem. We dared any man to interrupt our passionate claim to independence!

'At first I was afraid. I was petrified,
kept thinking I could never live without you by my side.
But then I spent so many nights thinking how you did me wrong.
And I grew strong and I learned how to get along.'

We sang the lyrics and my friend, Jodi, twirled me under her arm. Our voices grew stronger and louder as we recited the words:

'And so you're back, from outer space.
I just walked in to find you here with that sad look upon your face.
I should have changed that stupid lock; I should have made you leave your key.
If I'd have known for just one second you'd be back to bother me.
Go on now, go, walk out the door.
Just turn around now 'cause you're not welcome anymore.
Weren't you the one who tried to hurt me with goodbye?'

I rolled around the dance floor feeling liberated, brave, and sassy. The men sat this song out. The women of the club dominated this scene. We looked at the guys, pointing fingers and singing the song as if they were the ones to blame. We didn't dare miss this opportunity to bond together for a little women's movement.

'Did ya think I'd crumble?
Did ya think I'd lay down and die?
Oh no, not I. I will survive.
Oh as long as I know how to love, I know I'll stay alive.
I've got all my life to live. I've got all my love to give.
I'll survive. I will survive. Hey, hey.'

And just as the song said, I crumbled! I tumbled backwards while attempting to "pop a wheelie". My sassiness had gotten the best of me. My dancing had come to a tragic end as I lay on my back staring at the twirling disco ball that hung from the ceiling. My friends were there to pick me up. We laughed about it and they placed me upright. The real casualty was a broken finger. However, my shattered pride was more distressing. I was "break dancing", literally!

I continued dancing that night and the many weekends thereafter. I referred to this event as "my most embarrassing moment," but knew that this fall upon the dance floor held a lesson; a lesson for many. The moral of this story: Please get on the dance floor. Wheelchair or not, what's there to fear? No matter how awkward and clumsy it may feel, I guarantee it's been done before, and worse. If not for yourself, then dance for the sake of others. Wheelchair users are in a very unique position to show that we never have to give up the gift of dance or lose the spirit of life. That ought to get us all moving, even if Motown doesn't.

I choose to turn my most embarrassing moment into a teaching opportunity. Believe me; I know how tiresome the educational role wheelchair users are expected to play. But the dance floor was an easy way to demonstrate acceptance. All I had to do was dance.

I could change the deejay's perspective on disability, dance, and life. I could inspire a young man to dance with me, or maybe influence his decision to ask a wheelchair user on a date. What ever the case, my dancing is now a reputed dance for all those who choose to grab life and dance like there is no tomorrow! I just wish that it was this much fun to tear down all the other stereotypes. I'd dance my way through life; I'd be a dancing queen.

My ability to laugh at the situation made it unmistakably a night to remember. Falling isn't anything we plan. It usually happens. Something trips us up, sometimes causes us to stumble, sometimes making us fall flat on our backs. The important thing is that we get up. When I fell on the dance floor, it was because I became overconfident. It was laughter that got me up. Like any other challenges in life, it's important to understand that falling is par for the course. We must quickly recover and learn how to move forward. The two go together. So the next time you stumble, remember the lyrics from my favorite disco tune:

> *'It took all the strength I had not to fall apart,*
> *And tried so hard to mend the pieces of my broken heart.*
> *And I spent oh so many nights just feeling sorry for myself*
> *I used to cry, but now I hold my head up high,*
> *And you see me... somebody new,*
> *I'm not that chained up little person... Hey, hey.*
> **I will survive, I will survive!'**
> — *Lyrics by Gloria Gaynor*

Spirit, Body, and Mind

So then, those who suffer according to God's will should commit themselves
to their faithful Creator and continue to do good.
— 1 Peter 4:19

Spirit

Faith is believing in things unseen. Faith is the cornerstone of my spirit. I may be sitting down but I am standing firm on my faith.

The world in which we live is abundant with sophisticated wealth and possessions. Things that often create obsession — empty chattels in which we often search for validation and happiness. Yet, it is in the unseen where our greatest riches and freedom are found. I focus daily on my faith and sense the presence of God's hands in my life. I do not have to understand each event that unfolds; I merely accept that God will turn all the snapshots into one fabulous work of art. The only question I continually ask myself is, *"How does God want to use me today?"* And if you ask yourself this question, well, buckle up and grab tight! Your life is about to take off. And that's exactly what happened to mine. Oh, the places God has taken me.

Body

In order to be a faithful servant of God, I have to maintain my physical health. Nourishing my spirit, body, and mind is a constant requirement to stay balanced in my life. I work on myself in the gym, through prayer, and

The Miss Columbus Pageant.

in quiet time. The occasional trip to the local gym for aerobics is my favorite way to shake up my workout regimen. In fact, there was a time when I taught wheelchair aerobics. Twice a week, a group of ladies, all in wheelchairs, would meet at the gym and I would lead them through an upper body workout. We would share ideas with one another on how to improve our lives. The support we found in one another was priceless.

My workouts provide me with physical fitness and confidence. My level of injury affects my abdominal muscles. To offset my lack of abs, I have to wear a back brace. This provides me manageable stability. Weightlifting has provided increased strength in my arms, ultimately providing more independence.

Mind

We live in a society that has a narrow perception of beauty. The images that emerge from television and magazines influence our standards as a society, on which we measure attractiveness. One can easily believe that they have to be beautiful if they want to become a great person. But beauty seen by the eyes doesn't last forever, nor does it provide lasting contentment.

I have come to realize that the happiest people don't necessarily have the best of everything, including physical attractiveness. They just make the most of everything that comes their way, using adversities as stepping stones along the pathway of life.

My family joins me in a photo after the Miss Columbus Pageant: My sister, Terri, Mom, and niece, Brittany.

The brightest future will always be based on a forgotten past. In order to move forward in life one, must let go of the past and see beyond moments of pain and suffering.

This is exactly why I chose to enter the Miss Columbus Pageant. Already submerged in a society that underestimates my ability, I would now confront a spectacle that was known to typecast based on figures. In order to become Miss America, a contestant must first win a local competition. In my case, Miss Columbus was my local preliminary. Competition at any level of the Miss America Pageant Organization requires personal commitment, strong communication skills, and talent.

The idea of competing with eight other able-bodied women, in Evening Gown, Talent, Interview — and yes, *Swimsuit* — was a challenge where I may be unmatched; as an amateur in a wheelchair, could I complete with these seasoned professionals? Certainly the odds were against me, especially when it came time to showcase our level of fitness in bikinis. Nevertheless, I knew this was something I wanted to do, *something I needed to do*. The Miss Columbus Pageant would require me to compete in Artistic Expression (Talent); Presentation and Community Achievement (Interview); Presence and Poise (Eveningwear); and Lifestyle and Fitness (Swimsuit). The final night of competition would include the Lifestyle and Fitness portion; Presence and Poise; Peer Respect and Leadership; Artistic Expression; and Top Five Knowledge and Understanding competitions (provided by Miss America Organization official Web site). All these would be completed on stage in front of an audience expected to be two hundred or more.

As I prepared for the pageant, I soon realized that I was on a path that would be life- changing. As part of my training, I completed numerous mock interviews. The interview portion was crucial, weighing in at forty percent of total scoring. I had to be stunning and articulate. Every day I read the newspaper to sharpen my knowledge of current events. I read my Bible, to better express my love for Christ. I rehearsed questions ranging from my personal ambitions to my favorite foods. I became very clear in the message I wanted to convey. It all culminated into a simple message: Beauty is something that starts from within.

In the early summer of 1993, only a month after my high school graduation, the red curtain opened. On a lighted stage, I danced alongside eight intelligent, graceful, beautiful women, all aspiring to take home the crown. Elvis's number one hit, *Jailhouse Rock* played as we performed a country line dance in denim shirts and faded jeans. And Elvis himself made a special appearance. The impersonator put on an amusing presentation, only to fuel the nervousness and excitement that all the contenders felt.

The curtains closed and we rushed to our back stage dressing rooms for the first level of competition: *Swimsuit*. I had asked my lifelong friend, Dovie, for her assistance. We practiced for weeks, and she helped me find the quickest way to undress and re-dress from my wheelchair. It was not an easy task, but with strength and sheer determination, we did it in the allotted two-minute time frame.

I threw off my shirt, and then my tight denim jeans, not caring at all where they landed in my dressing room. At the same time, Dovie grabbed masking tape and began wrapping it around my waist (an old trick of the pageant trade). It was nice to find out that what I had thought were "perfect" bodies often were the making of a masking tape masterpiece. The swimsuit fit tight, and with the help of the tape, my body was transformed. With a quick lipstick refresh and swab of Vaseline on my teeth (another trick — it makes it easier to smile), I took a deep breath and rolled onto the stage.

The host announced my interests and hobbies. I smiled and twirled along the catwalk, pausing for a moment to make eye contact with the judges. It seemed like time stood still. The only saving grace was the bright spotlight. The light was so blinding that it prevented me from seeing beyond the first row. I imagined that they were the only people in the room. As I rolled off the stage, the crowd cheered — a sobering reminder that there *was* a crowd.

The worst was over. From this point on, I knew I could enjoy myself. But I had to remain focused; the next wardrobe change was more complex. I had to get into a blue beaded dress and arrange my thoughts for the talent portion. It was important to secure a strong performance; it would be thirty percent of my score. Unfortunately, my choices for talent were limited. Tap dancing or the Rumba was, of course, out of the question, and the only place I ever sang was in the shower and on the dance floor. With no musical talent whatsoever, I was left with my skill as a writer. I wrote a monologue, *The Body can never tie down the Soul.*

As the contestant before me finished her rendition of *Crazy* by Patsy Cline, I thought, *I must be the crazy one.* It was too late, however, to turn back. I had to finish what I started. The host introduced me and music accompanied my monologue:

> *"Live life to the fullest and find joy in each day.*
> *Be true to yourself and find the strength to carry on.*
> *Find a purpose in everything you do.*
> *And discover, even in adversity, a life that you have dreamed of."*

I dramatically recited my work from memory. I was blessed to have a large group of supporters in the audience. They cheered and waved handmade signs that read, "Go get 'em Leslie." Their love and encouragement was far more precious than a crown. But in my moment of gratitude, I pulled my thoughts together for the last and final performance, Evening Wear.

In this wardrobe change, we had an extra two minutes, giving us time to change into high heels and pantyhose and for a quick hair redo. By now, Dovie and I worked like clockwork. During my talent presentation, she had prepared my evening gown and paired up my jewelry. She looked at me and smiled. "Leslie, you are great out there. You really have a shot at this." Her words ran through me like sweet wine. Her confidence in me gave me a sense of reassurance that I was here for a reason. It was in that moment that I closed my eyes and took pleasure in the experience. Eighty percent of my score had been calculated.

In 1989, the Miss America Organization introduced the platform concept as part of the competition. It requires all contestants to select an issue that she would like to support. Contestants are scored on the importance and relevance of the topic and how it relates to our nation. The curtains lifted for the last time of the evening. I gracefully rolled onto stage in a ruby red beaded gown. I positioned myself in front of the audience, reached for the microphone, and shared my selected platform. I lost any inhibitions and boldly said, "It has been an honor to be a participant in the Miss Columbus Pageant." I continued on, "This journey has been an experience where I set out to prove inner strength and confidence are the essence of beauty. I encourage you all to find your passions and pursue them. For your dreams will lead you to your destiny. If I am so lucky to represent my hometown as Miss Columbus, I would dedicate my time to help women discover their strengths. I would use my experiences to help promote strong self awareness, teaching women how to overcome life's obstacles. My speech may end here, but my voyage has just begun. And, what a worthwhile journey it is. Take with you my gratitude for allowing me to share a glimpse of who I am. Truly, you can see that beauty begins from within."

I felt an immense sense of satisfaction. I loved the sound of my voice bouncing back with the affirming applaud. I knew I had done my best. It was up to the judges and their perspective to determine how well I portrayed grace, poise, and stage presence.

Earlier that day, we had a chance to vote for the contestant who most deserved to be Miss Congeniality. I voted for a close friend of mine. She was full of spunk and spirit. Kim Dickerson was a portrait of a woman with power. Strong, determined, yet graceful and compassionate. She was well-deserving of the reward. I expected no other name than Miss Kimberly Dickerson. "And Miss Congeniality goes to Miss Leslie Taylor." *Did he say my name?* Everyone smiled. I hugged the girls to my left and right, and rolled to the announcer who gave me a beautiful silver platter. What a wonderful token for a wonderful evening.

The announcer went on to announce the runners-up. "Forth runner up goes to…," and a beautiful woman standing about five foot eight received an armful of roses. "Third runner-up is…" "Second runner up… Miss Leslie Taylor." I was stunned. I had never expected to place, much less to be awarded a prestigious title such as this.

Becoming Miss Congeniality and second runner-up was an achievement like no other. It took several days for me to completely absorb what I accomplished. I was the first contestant in a wheelchair to compete and place ahead of these seasoned pageant contenders. It was a milestone. I was asked by local newspapers, media shows, and surrounding schools for interviews and speaking engagements. During the competition I said, "In pursuit of your passions your destiny will be found." I embraced this idea as I developed a passion for the stage. I recalled, *If I had listened to the fears in my head and did not chase this dream with the passion of my heart, I would have never known this humbling exhilaration.* I had started this experience with the question of how to live a life of substance and beauty? I finished with a deeper understanding of my truest self. I also found a love for speaking. The pageant had forced me to face many of my fears and anguish that come with being a quadriplegic. My presentation about tragedy and overcoming had become a great source of healing for me, and hopefully, for my audiences as well. This experience sparked the yearning for continuation of sharing my testimony.

"And Jesus came and spoke unto them saying, all power is given unto me in heaven and earth. Go, therefore, and teach all nations, baptizing them in the name of the Father , and the Son, and the Holy Spirit, teaching them to

observe all things what so ever I have commanded you. And I am with you
always. Even until the end of time."
-Matthew 28:18-20

We are to go-whether God calls us to breakdown stereotypes in a pageant or to go next door to encourage a neighbor-we are to go. It is not an option but a command to all that serve the Lord. We all have a part in fulfilling God's great commission. It starts with us making ourselves available for God to use.

I could of never found the strength on my own to compete in a *"beauty pageant"*. It was the confidence that I found in Jesus that propelled me across the stage. It was out of discipleship that I spoke of my faith during the grueling ten minute interview.

If you study the Bible, you'll find that its pages are full of tribulation and hardships. There are stories of unfulfilled dreams. There are stories of those who never lost faith in the midst of adversities. Think of Paul, Job, and Joseph. Ultimately God changed their lives and used their hardships to refine their Christian attributes. They became strong and developed a steadfast spirit that reflected the image of God. I believe that God still uses our challenges to refine our faith. I believe, too, that He wants to fulfill our dreams. It might not be in the way we anticipate, but if we seek God's intent for our lives, the adventure will change us. God wants people who are willing to say, "Lord God, I am committed to obeying You, regardless of the circumstances."

Something to Remember

I received so much encouragement. Word traveled quickly about me, and people were eager to offer words of advice, local sponsorship, and support. But the most treasured friendship I developed was with a queen.

Surrounding pageant titleholders often traveled to attend preliminary meets. They would sit in the audience studying each contestant's talent and stage presentations. After the night's activities were completed, the contestants had a chance to meet all the titleholders and ask questions. Although the pageants were very competitive, there were times where the girls would share ideas on how to better perform — to thrive — in their competitions.

I had the unique opportunity to meet Miss Cullman Area, Heather Whitestone, a beautiful lady who immediately encouraged me to continue to remove barriers for the challenged. She spoke so elegantly. Heather explained that she just recently won her preliminary. Like me, she had to overcome her own obstacles. Heather lost her hearing when she was eighteen months of age. A severe reaction to a diphtheria-tetanus vaccine caused her to become deathly ill. In an attempt to save her life, doctors gave her antibiotics. Unfortunately, the medicines caused nerve damage in her ears, resulting in deafness. Whitestone's hearing was amplified with a hearing aid, and she was taught to speak through the Acoupedics approach, an educational technique designed to teach the deaf to speak, as well as use sign language.

That night, after my pageant debut, we talked and encouraged one another. It was amazing to find out that she set out to compete in her respective pageant with the same expectations as mine: To prove there is more within a person with a disability. We promised to keep in touch.

A few weeks later, I received a letter from Heather. "When I watched you on stage I had the feeling that we experienced the same feeling. I believe we had the same obstacles and we have responsibilities to overcome. I'm glad that you learned that pageants are not about winning a crown, but winning new lifelong friends. But you know what? I'm sure it's your essence that makes the pageants meaningful. I still believe you can win," she wrote. I placed her letter on my dresser mirror where it provided me encouragement time and time again.

That year Heather went on to win her state title, Miss Alabama. And then on the evening of September 14, 1994, on national television, I watched Heather Whitestone become Miss America. She was the first deaf Miss America. In fact, she was the first woman with a physical challenge to win the crown. I will never forget when they announced her name. Her expression did not change. It wasn't until the runner-up pointed to her and Heather read her lips, *"It's you. You're Miss America."*

No person was more suited for the title. The expectations that were placed on Heather were overwhelming, yet she handled all the pressures of a queen with style, assurance, and steadfast strength.

As Miss America, Heather traveled the nation promoting her **STARS** program (**S**uccess **T**hrough **A**ction and **R**ealization of your dream**s**), encouraging women to stand for their dreams, to not be passive in life's mission.

We still keep in touch and our friendship provides me with the reassurance that I am never alone. Her dedication to Christ and her ability to disciple are always evident. She taught me so many things. Above all, I learned that there are many who walk the path of adversity.

The Pageants Continue

A passion had been ignited within me. I wanted to compete again. Ms. Wheelchair America was a forum designed for the promotion of the achievements of people with mobility impairments. It is a nonprofit program that is staffed and coordinated by volunteers throughout the country dedicated to increasing public awareness through education and service. It was the natural course to my pageant pursuit.

Disabilities were varied, ranging from cerebral palsy to muscular dystrophy. All were pulled together by a familiar thread: our wheelchairs. I knew that this was part of my destiny, part of God's plan. I had that feeling you get when you are in tune with a cause greater than yourself, like I was synchronized in harmony with a grander plan.

For five days, each contestant shared our ambitions, thoughts, and beliefs with the panel of judges. We were asked about law reform, politics, and questioned on the impact of the ADA (Americans with Disability Act). The pressure of being well-spoken, well-versed, and well-informed demanded unvarying intensity and was mentally exhausting. My core frame of mind throughout competition was fidelity — truth to myself and devotion to my purpose.

The competition was located in my hometown; daily interviews were held at the host hotel. Between interviews, we fellowshipped, had luncheons, and enjoyed themed dinners. The last night of competition was at the Liberty Theatre, known for its historical singers like "Ma" Rainey. The restoration of this landmark was long awaited. We were honored to be celebrated as the first performers. The modernized stage, although brand new, held a charm influenced by the rich legacy of Southern tradition.

This competition was not a "beauty" pageant. It was a forum to select the most accomplished and articulate spokesperson to represent the millions of Americans with disabilities. The judging criteria stress that Ms. Wheelchair Georgia not a beauty contest, but points out that the winner should have *"a pleasing appearance capable of obtaining favorable responses from any audience."* The selected delegate would be required to represent the state of Georgia in the Miss Wheelchair America Pageant that follows the same guidelines.

As we waited behind the red curtain, I secretly studied each woman's face. To my left was Judy, a high-level quadriplegic. Her injury had affected her ability to use her arms and hands. She wore a beautiful white dress with small gold beads, perfectly placed to draw attention to the curves of her angelic face. She used a "sip and blow" power chair — a wheelchair design with high-tech mechanics that enabled Judy to steer and propel her wheelchair with the slightest sip or blow of her breaths. To my right was Tracey, a young vibrant woman. She whispered to me, "My hands are shaking. Are yours?" As I looked down at her quivering hands, I saw a small angel pinned to the upholstery of her wheelchair. "You'll do great," I said. "You've got your guardian with you." I pointed to the silver pin and smiled. I knew that every woman on this stage had overcome so much to be here. I was in the presence of amazing women. What a task it would be for the judges to choose only one winner. As far as I was concerned, just to be in this place was victorious.

Along with our military escorts, in their dress blues, we danced to another Motown favorite of mine, *Celebration*. We had decorated our wheelchairs with beads, rhinestones, and tinsel. The parade of women in eveningwear and decked out wheelchairs would have made Jennifer Lopez jealous! We had more jewels than Tiffany & Company. It was over the top; our presentation was an expression of our unbreakable spirits.

An evening filled with entertainers and inspiring stories came to a conclusion with the crowning of a queen. On May 17, 1997, a sash was placed around my shoulder and a tiara upon my head. In that moment, I assigned the responsibility of representing the achievements of many women. It was a duty I did not enter into lightly. Upon my head I wore a crown, but upon my heart I wore a promise I would carry out. Tears of joy rolled down my face as I saw my family, friends, and colleagues as they celebrated with me. We finished the evening with a dance and dinner at the hotel. All the contestants shared in my excitement.

The following morning I was asked to give my first speech as Ms. Wheelchair Georgia. I selected my words carefully. "I am grateful to sit before you today and proudly take on my duties as your Ms. Wheelchair Georgia. I will make it my personal responsibility to use this opportunity to promote and further the greatness of women with disabilities. It is my hope that you recognize your own milestone. Use this experience as your reflection for personal growth. We owe it to ourselves to celebrate today and aspire to accomplish great things tomorrow. It doesn't take a crown or a title to prove you are a winner; just the willingness to step out and demonstrate that you are willing to make a difference. May your journey be filled with passion, conviction, and faith."

Although the crown I received as Ms. Wheelchair Georgia was rewarding it was no reflection to the crown I was given when I first accepted Christ in my life. I will never forget the day that I was baptized and I was lifted out as a born again Christian. I was young, nine years old, but I knew the importance of this day because God had pressed upon my heart the promise of everlasting life. I was given a crown that I did not have to compete for nor could it ever be taken away from me. The price had been paid upon the cross and God had sent his only begotten son to die for me ad forgive me of my sins. Looking back it's amazing to me how my immature mind and lack if life experiences did not hinder me from completely understanding the concept of God's love for me.

I saw my title as Ms. Wheelchair Georgia as a unique opportunity to lead others to the crown of everlasting life. In my travels as Ms. Wheelchair Georgia, I went to churches, civic groups, fund raisers and corporate meetings sharing my testimony-spreading my love of Jesus. I had the chance to meet many influential people, from the State Senator to the corporate presidents. And yet it wasn't any designated official that stood out in my mind. It was people like Anna. She was a college student who was paralyzed from the neck down. She, too, was forced to live life sitting down.

One day I read a comment she posted to her fellow wheelchair friends on a support group chat room. She wrote, "Today was a good day for me. My favorite music video was played several times on CMT. I danced in my head and vividly recalled the freedom I found in dance. I even managed to bounce my shoulders a little to the rhythm of the music. How I love to dream of the day I will dance again." Prior her injury, Anna was an accomplished theatrical dancer. She was on a full dance scholarship at the Art Institute of Los Angeles.

Her vulnerability and honesty touched me deeply. I saw her, not as a person in need, but a woman with a dream. She is someone who remembers that to be free and to dream are worth having above many other things. In fact, in some ways, Anna might be even more in touch with her dreams. Many of us live at such an intense pace that we leave little time for dreaming. Anna had not forgotten what it is like to dream. Her perspective had not become as gray as her surroundings; Anna still had hope.

This story made me question: *Why do some people, against all odds, still hold to the dreams in their heart and others allow their dreams to be crushed beyond recognition?* I can only answer this from my personal experiences. I must admit that for years, I allowed things to keep me from my passions and dreams. Although other commitments hold importance in my life, had I forgotten how important it was to experience the pleasure of pursuing my God-given talents?

Take a moment to think about your own life. What did you dream when you were young? How have your dreams changed? Did you choose to lay them down, or did circumstances force you to give them up? Do you even remember what they were? What happened to your dreams?

It's so easy to say that there is no time for dreaming; that aspirations are left only for those whose only responsibility is to care for themselves. Thoughts and assumptions like this put limitations on the joy we allow ourselves to seek in life. What constraints have we held onto that make laughter trivial and dreaming a thing of the past? It wasn't until months after becoming Ms. Wheelchair Georgia that I would truly discover the words I had just spoken at my first speech would be my own motivation in my life's greatest adventures. I would need the ability to dream, have passion, conviction, and faith.

After competing in both pageant circuits, Miss. America preliminary and Ms. Wheelchair Georgia, I witnessed the harsh reality of drastic differences in the support each pageant received. While the Miss America system was successful in gaining corporate sponsorship- *providing enough funding to cover the expense of pageant production, establish a scholarship fund for the winner, provide a staff for the winner during her reign, and provide exciting prizes.* Whereas the Ms. Wheelchair Organization operates on a slight travel budget, winners arrange their engagements in their spare time, and with no professional staff to help. The entire pageant functions on volunteers and depends upon the hard work from contestants themselves. Sponsorship money and entry fees are solely the contestant's responsibility. It made me question, Are the physically challenged still being over looked as a viable source of commercial revenue? You would think that corporate sponsors would be knocking the door down to have the opportunity to support such a great organization that represents the more than 11,000 people that become disabled every year. How far we have really come? It's just proof that there is still a lot more work to do.

Friends

This is how we know what love is; Jesus laid down his life for us. And we ought to lay down our lives for our brothers.
— 1 John 3:16

The Pennsylvania ski slope was covered in a thick layer of snow and ice. It was beautiful. I was eager to get into the bi-ski for the first time. I read about skiing in sports magazines for people with disabilities, but I never imagined that I would have the opportunity to try it out. Randy Golden, my friend and employer, was determined to expose me to new adventures. "Now, Leslie, if you don't want to do this, you don't have to. Are you sure this is what you want to do?" Randy asked me for the third time. "I'm sure, Randy. You just prepare to be out-skied." I laughed. Randy smiled, "All right, let's do it."

We said very little on the ski lift. The bitter cold practically dazed us. My mind replayed out the directions of the instructor. As our point of exit came closer, the instructor told Randy how he could assist in get-
ting me and the bi-ski off the lift. My job was simply to hang on. They counted to three and up we went; to my amazement, Randy and the instructor safely balanced me between the two of them and gently placed me on the packed snow. The weather conditions were fierce as more ice, and less snow, began to fall. The good news was there were not many skiers on the slope, which meant fewer people for me to injure on my way down.

As the slope gradually became steeper, the speed of my ski increased. I traveled

Aaron is positively my best friend.

about fifty feet and thought to myself, *I can do this. It's easier than I thought it would be.* As soon as that thought entered my mind, the ski began swaying side to side and then, out of control. Suddenly, I was face down in the frigid snow. Randy, of course, was the first one to my side. As he rolled my ski back over, he asked, "Les, you alright?" With a big grin on my face, I shouted, "Haven't been better. This is awesome!" For the first time, I experienced a total adrenaline rush from a sport! I was overwhelmed with excitement and knew I would forever love to ski. At this point, I wasn't interested in learning techniques or the right way to ski, I was just interested in having fun. For that entire day, my runs down the mountain were a lot like my first run. Fifty or seventy feet and down I went. Randy would roll me back over and off we would go, only to fall again. As the sun sank behind the mountains, we found refuge in the lodge, where a crackling fire warmed our frigid bodies. I exhausted Randy, and I'm certain my instructor was frustrated with my inability to follow his instruction and learn techniques for better skiing. He probably thought I was un-teachable.

The lodge was filled with wheelchairs of all shapes and sizes. The colors and wheels were just as endless as the people who occupied them. This ski camp was an annual event and drew people from all over the country. It was hosted by HealthSouth Rehabilitation Center. The camp's mission was to promote the awareness of adaptive skiing. It was an opportunity for professional athletes to demonstrate their skills as well as provide a venue for people to try the sport. Randy brought me to market his company's urological products and to support the camp as a corporate sponsor.

As I began to take off the layer of jackets I was wearing, I noticed a young man approaching me. Our eyes met and we exchanged smiles. "Nice wheels babe," he said. I smiled and thought, *What a line. At least he is original.* He introduced himself, "My name is Aaron." He went on to explain that he was the lead instructor for the camp and apologized that he was pressed for time. "If you give me your name and number, I would like to get to know you." He handed a magazine to me. On the cover was a "tricked out" downhill mountain bike. I looked at the cover with amazement. "That's my buddy, Darol. He's a paraplegic, and there's an article inside about him and his mountain bike. Keep the magazine today and I'll get it from you tomorrow. Just make sure you write your number inside the front cover." He winked at me and disappeared in the crowd of people.

He was gorgeous — dark expressive eyes, a masculine shadow of a beard — his appearance was tough and rugged. Why did he want my number? He couldn't possibly be interested in me. He was out of my league. I flipped through the magazine.

After Randy and I recuperated from our downhill skiing adventure, we made our way to the social event. I was extremely tired, but Randy felt like we had to make an appearance. I spent the entire night looking for Aaron. *Who was this guy, and why was he interested in staying in touch with me?* After two hours of talking with new friends and making business connections, we returned to our cabins and got a good night's rest.

Early the next morning, there he was, this tall, strong, mystifying man. I watched him from across the room. He helped a young man adjust his footrest on his wheelchair, shook the gentleman's hand and went on his way. I found an open space at a table near a window that overlooked the ski slope. I stared out at the beautiful mountain.

I had not yet learned of Aaron's intentions, yet I found myself wondering about him. Too many times before I had emotionally fallen too fast, only to discover someone who was not mature enough to understand the scope of my disability. Why did I think this guy was going to be any different?

"Hey, did you read the article about my friend?" I was startled. I was so caught up in my thoughts that Aaron's approach had come as a surprise. *What did I do with that magazine?* My heart was racing and my eyes were absorbed by this mysterious man. "The magazine — I haven't had a chance to read the article yet", I replied in a soft voice. *Why did he make me so nervous?* I was usually sure of myself around men, but at this moment I felt like a young school girl who just met her first crush. "I left the magazine in the equipment room yesterday. I'll get for you now." Aaron followed. As I handed it to him, he opened the cover and said, "You forgot to write your phone number."

With some hesitation, I wrote my number in the magazine, marked with a heart. *What a cliché — I was worse than lovesick puppy.* "Thank you. I can't wait to get to know you better. I've always wanted to meet a real Georgia peach!" And with that Aaron, disappeared. After three days of downhill skiing, I was ready to return to the mild temperatures back home. I resumed my regular routine at work.

Randy was such a great boss. He told everyone in the office about my skiing experience and, of course, found every opportunity to give me a hard time about making him ski in such harsh conditions. I would always come back at him, reminding him that big boys don't cry. I was passionate about my career. I felt like my work with MMG Healthcare was part of my purpose. My experiences and struggles as a quadriplegic were put to use every day. I would often have the opportunity to share my story with the newly injured and soon found myself in a position that helped change the future for many.

Randy had a project and needed my assistance. The project's objective was to show grassroots government the need for law reform regarding issues on Medicare reimbursement for products that directly affect the quality of life for persons with spinal cord injuries. MMG Healthcare was an amazing company. Situated in a suburb of Atlanta, occupying over 10,000 square feet of space, with a team of more than 300, we manufactured and distributed urological products that were used by people with bladder dysfunction. From the young to old, injured or non-injured, our products were essential to the health of many people. One unique product was designed to lower chronic illness and reduce the cases of infections among catheter users. The family-owned business began at the kitchen table of the Golden's house. John, Randy's father, had a vision that one day the company would grow and become a leader in the industry, and the O'Neil Catheter was the product that would take them there.

As we worked closely with local, state, and eventually national legislation, we began to see that this task would not be easy. Our goal was to get Medicare to change its reimbursement rate for the O'Neil Catheter. So many people needed this product, but few had the financial resources to obtain it. I became fully engaged in my work. The days at the office grew longer as I spent countless hours on the phone. I began to educate our customers and urged them to write letters of support to their state representatives. Late one afternoon Randy informed me that he secured a meeting with a National Representative in Washington, D.C. If we could get Washington's support, new legislation would be introduced that could potentially change Medicare billing. We were optimistic.

That night I returned to my studio apartment, a small 900 square foot space with outrageously expensive rent, furnished with hand-me-downs. There was not much to it, but it was my home. I was proud of my accomplishments and independence. I wasn't there long when the phone rang. I thought to myself, *It must be my momma.* She always called around the same time to make sure I made it in safely. I was so sure it was she that I answered with a sweet, "Hi, Mom." "No, this is Aaron." Then, a long pause. "Aaron, from the ski camp. Do you remember who I am?" the strong sultry voice on the other end replied. My heart began to race and my stomach quickly turned into a million knots. With a calm voice, I replied, "Yes, I remember you." I tried not to show my excitement and surprise by his call. We talked for more than three hours that night. We shared our ambitions, likes, and dislikes. We laughed together and ended our conversations with a promise to talk again the next day.

That night it was difficult to fall asleep. I still did not understand why Aaron had such an emotional effect on me, but he did. I made up my mind, long before I met him, that there was no room in my life for a relationship now. My focus was my work. Yet, I couldn't get Aaron off my mind.

For the next three weeks, Aaron and I spoke on the phone every night. With each conversation, I grew to know and respect the man he was. At work, the Medicare project came to an end when government legislation was reformed and Medicare criteria for reimbursement was changed. The new legislation made it easier for more people to obtain the O'Neil Catheter and ultimately live healthier lives. The entire staff celebrated. Both John and Randy congratulated me on my dedication to the project and rewarded me with a nice pay increase. The Goldens made me feel like I was part of their family, and I knew that this was where I wanted to be. As I shared the great news with Aaron, he asked me if I would consider going on a date with him. "I would love to go on a date with you. But how is this going to work with 500 miles between us?" I asked. Aaron proceeded to tell me that his close friend, Danny, was celebrating his thirtieth birthday. He wanted me to fly to Washington. There he would pick me up and we would travel to Fredericksburg, Virginia.

Until now, I felt our relationship was safe. In our conversations, we were friends getting to know one another. A trip to his hometown would be a huge risk. A weekend with me would reveal the unpleasant realities of my life. I'm sure my life as a quadriplegic would be too much for him to handle. He could certainly spend his time with an able-bodied woman who had less baggage than I. A date with Aaron would require me to leave my safe comfort zone.

Would I indulge myself in something that could lead to a great relationship? Or would I hide in the dark shadows of doubt and loneliness?

I told him that I needed a few days to answer. I quickly ended our conversation. *Was the risk worth taking?* I knew very little about Aaron — the only details I knew were the ones he shared with me in our nightly phone calls. I desperately wanted to continue this friendship, but I was apprehensive, to say the least.

My dating life until this point was not typical. When I was a sophomore, I met Daniel, a charming and friendly young man. What started out as a friendship grew into a four-year relationship. I felt safe. Over time, I shared the differences in my life with my boyfriend. It was difficult for me to imagine that there could be anyone else who would understand my adversity. Daniel accepted me as I was.

But we were young and had a lot to learn about life, love, and independence. After graduation, our lives began to take separate paths. Soon we found ourselves in different places with different goals. The breakup was devastating. I convinced myself that Daniel was my one shot at love, and when he left, there would be no one else.

Dating after high school proved to be more challenging; the safety I felt from a long-term relationship was gone. I quickly detached from the dating scene and became committed to my career. A relationship was something I was just not ready for. I did not want to expose my weakness or share my disability with anyone else. It had been too exhausting and painful in the past.

Somehow, after much thought and debate, I found the strength to take the chance. I flew to Virginia and met Aaron. He greeting me at the airport with a long-stemmed red rose. He was more stunning than I remembered. As we drove to his parents' house, he said, "I bought a CD to listen to." I was impressed; I thought it would a love ballad to set the mood for a romantic weekend. It was bluegrass! I laughed uncontrollably. Here we were on our first date and we were jamming to what sounded like the theme song of *Hee Haw*. I just knew Aaron was a good ole' boy!

Aaron may have missed the mark on his choice of date music, but he more than made up for it when he pointed out a special surprise he had for me. In order to assure that my wheelchair could maneuver in his parents' house, Aaron reconstructed several doorways. The bathroom door was a standard twenty-four-inch door. His experience working with the disabled taught him this would be a tight squeeze for my wheelchair. He took down the door framing, cut into the sheetrock, and reframed a wider door! I could not believe what I was seeing. The fact that someone took the initiative to make my life easier for just one weekend was astonishing! I knew I was in the company of an incredible man.

Despite my desire to keep my heart guarded, I felt my emotions surface. *What woman could deny this sincere act of kindness and compassion?* I just prayed that Aaron would be willing to accept me just as I am.

Now it was great to have a bathroom that was accessible for my wheelchair, but the average bathroom is not accessible to me. Here I was, in the parents house of a man I was interested in building a relationship with. There were obvious bathroom challenges I had to figure out independently. When it came time to shower, I successfully transferred. But getting back out was a complication. After technically trying to lift, pull, and push my out of the tub, I literally crawled out by means of the shower curtain.

There I lie, exhausted, on the bathroom floor, in the house of newly meet folks. Suddenly I heard the screech of the door and there was Bonnie, Aaron's mom staring right at me. She graciously said, "Excuse me, I was just checking on you." I don't think she was prepared at all to see me floundering around on the floor. She sweetly asked if I need any assistance. She then smiled with a hit of humor and said, "You look like a little mermaid." Although this moment for me was quite embarrassing, it marked the beginning of a great relationship with Bonnie and I. She came to see and understand the drastic differences in my life.

Horse-Drawn Carriage

Many waters cannot quench love, neither can the floods drown it: if a man would give all the substance of his house for love, it would utterly be contemned.
— *Song of Solomon 8:7*

During the next six months Aaron and I saw each other every weekend. Although he lived in Fredericksburg, Virginia, we managed to spend the weekends together. On Fridays Aaron would pack up his truck and leave his job as a prosthetic technician. It would take him twelve hours to reach my apartment in Atlanta. Often it wouldn't be until Saturday morning before he made it to my apartment.

We spent every moment together. I took him to my favorite restaurants and we went out with friends. Randy requested that we visit every time Aaron was in town. Aaron and Randy had common interests. They talked about football, saltwater fish tanks, and sports cars. Randy treated us like royalty. He invited us, along with his girlfriend Fiona, to dinner and a show downtown. We sat in the back of his car, sunroof open, and admired the beautiful Atlanta skyline. Aaron and I soaked up every moment we had together; our weekends would come to an end all too quickly.

In September, Aaron and I planned a trip to my hometown, Columbus. It was my birthday and my mom wanted to help celebrate the occasion. Aaron planned a great dinner and prepared a home-cooked meal for my mom, sister, and me. He asked me to dress nicely because after dinner we were going downtown for a special surprise. As we left my mother's house, she hugged Aaron's neck and thanked him for the special dinner. She sent us off with a smile and blew a kiss to me.

"Aaron, where are you taking me?" I asked. "You'll see. Just be patient my dear," he smiled. Aaron was always full of surprises. We had grown very close and we shared our deepest hopes, fears, and ambitions. Yet,

Aaron always maintained a sense of mystery. He found it easy to talk about his future, his plans, and his life, but struggled in sharing words of affirmation. I often questioned his true feelings for me, but I convinced myself that he must be crazy about me if he spent twelve hours driving — one way — to spend time with me. It had been weeks since I knew I fell in love with him. Actually, I fell for him on that first date and my love grew with each passing day. I was aching to tell him my true feelings, but it was only proper for the man to tell the woman first. How desperately I wanted to hear him say those three words!

Once we arrived to the Historic District, Aaron pushed me along a cobblestone road. He pointed to a park bench and we sat together quietly, hand in hand. *Clip, clop. Clip, clop.* I looked over my shoulder and behind us was a horse-drawn carriage pulled by a beautiful white stallion. The horse's hooves struck the cobblestone road with force.

"Are you ready?" And before I had a chance to answer, Aaron swept me up in his arms and placed me in the carriage. There lay a dozen long-stemmed red roses.

The carriage slowly strolled through the Historic District. Most of the houses dated back to the 1800s, and their charm was abundant. The carriage driver told us stories of the past and pointed out the home of Dr. Pemberton, the founder of the original Coca Cola formula. The tour ended as we gazed over the Chattahoochee River and the Dillingham Street Bridge, a local landmark. The breeze gently blew my hair, and the crisp evening air gave me a slight chill. I indulged in the moment and loved the way Aaron's arms felt around me. I felt safe.

Aaron took my hand and fell to one knee. "Leslie, will you marry me?" I heard a hint of uncertainty in his voice. His strong hands shook nervously as he displayed a lovely diamond ring. Entranced, perplexed, and somewhat confused, I struggled to absorb what was unfolding before me.

Marry him? What? How could I get married? When I'm dating, I can hide a lot of the "ugly" things about my disability. Aaron knew me pretty well by now, but marriage? *How could I keep a man like Aaron interested in me forever? How would I manage a family? Could I even have a family? Oh, and what about sex?* Bewildered, my mind raced in a million directions. There was so much to consider.

I knew, long before this day, that I wanted to spend my life with Aaron, but I never knew he wanted the same. His proposal was unexpected.

I leaned down, pulled him close to me and whispered, "You know this is forever; forever with me. You know that my life is different, very different." I sounded as if I was almost trying to talk him out of the proposal! He nodded "yes" and asked once more, "Will you marry me?" I was surprised when the words rolled off my lips, "Yes, I will marry you."

In that moment, it seemed nothing else existed around us. The river disappeared. The horse and carriage seemed to vanish, and the only sensation I felt was the touch of Aaron's hands as he slid the diamond ring on my finger. I felt safe — I felt sure — and I knew that Aaron was the man God chose for me.

Throughout our engagement, Aaron and I discussed the details of how our lives together would unfold. We first thought Aaron would move to Atlanta and find employment. I was established in my career and wanted to continue my work with MMG Healthcare. Aaron was flexible. In fact, he said, "If you were in China I would follow you there."

Without hesitation, he said goodbye to his family and friends, and moved to the South. It didn't take long before Aaron grew to enjoy Southern hospitality and traditional foods. Chicken and dumplings, Southern-fried chicken, and black-eyed peas became favorites of his; he often requested that my mother prepare these meals. Of course, she graciously obliged, forcing Aaron to go on a diet. We settled into a life together and began preparations for our wedding day.

I dreamed of my wedding many times. I wanted to feel like a princess. I envisioned a white wedding dress with a long train — a traditional wedding in my church with loved ones there to witness the exchange of vows. Aaron and I agreed the wedding should be a reflection of who we are. Together, we planned our special day.

On March 30, 1998, Aaron and I were married at Wynnbrook Baptist Church in my hometown, Columbus, Georgia. The day was perfect. With the assistance of Pastor Brad Hicks, we wrote our vows. Despite a rainstorm, 275 guests attended. We had eight attendants on each side, specially selected to honor treasured friendships.

Surprising to many of our guests, out of the sixteen attendants, four groomsmen had disabilities. Through Aaron's experience as an adaptive ski instructor, he was blessed with the friendships of these four amazing men.

Darol, a paraplegic, and passionate about sports, met Aaron in Vail, Colorado. Together they improved techniques and teaching styles that advanced the sport of adaptive skiing. Aaron would often ski beside Darol in a mono-ski. This helped Aaron understand how the equipment performed and helped him improve his teaching style.

Danny, a paraplegic, met Aaron on the slopes. A committed friend to Aaron, he always found laughter in every situation. Moments before our wedding ceremony, Danny's cross bars on his wheelchair broke in half. With no time to spare, Aaron retrieved duct tape from his truck and quickly repaired the broken frame. It was Danny's thirtieth birthday party where Aaron took me to Virginia for our first date.

Anthony, an amputee, had tried his hand at adaptive skiing before. He enjoyed skiing with his family, prior the loss of his left leg in a car collision. It was only natural for him to be drawn to the sport. Time after time, Anthony worked with instructors, but found it difficult to make turns. Aaron discovered that Anthony's weight was off balance due to his missing limb and solved this problem by placing a large rock inside the mono-ski, securing it to the left side. The rock anchored the weight difference, providing Anthony the ability to carve turns as he swiftly descended down the ski slope. The rock was eventually replaced with specialized lead weights. Today the famous rock sits on Anthony's bookshelf with the inscription, "The Anchor."

Christopher, a family friend of Aaron's, was our ring bearer. Although I don't think he approved of our marriage, he graciously participated in our wedding. I reassured Christopher that his relationship with Aaron would be the same and there was no need to worry about their summer Switzerland trips; Aaron still planned to continue their annual trips together.

The wedding was made special by these four men, and I would come to respect them for the relentless ways each of them dealt with their respective disabilities.

My bridesmaids were also close and dear to my heart. I was blessed to have two maids of honor: my sister, Terri, and my high school friend, Dovie. Their friendships had been critical to my growth and impacted my life beyond comprehension. My seven bridesmaids consisted of my family and dear friends, three of whom I had known since birth. Jodi, Heather, and Tiffany, my childhood friends, had been part of many memories of play, discovery, and equality. The unconditional love they shared with me was a contributing factor to the development of my self-esteem and confidence. Next, Brittany, Alexis, and Lisa, the next generation in my family. I was fortunate to know them as children and was blessed with the opportunity to watch them grow into beautiful young adults. Alexis, Aaron's younger sister, would now become part of my family. The circle of love and support provided by these men and women will remain a driving force in our lives.

The morning of our wedding was spent at the church. Preparations were made and I fellowshipped with my bridesmaids. Prior to the ceremony, Jason, Aaron's brother, knocked on the door and asked to see me. I wheeled into the hallway to see Jason standing there with an armful of roses. "A dozen red roses for you, Leslie. They're from Aaron," he explained. My eyes filled with tears.

For the next two hours, every half hour, a dozen long-stemmed red roses would appear. Each bouquet was delivered by one of Aaron's groomsmen. The final dozen was sweetly delivered by Aaron's dad, Rex. He whispered, "It's great to have you become part of our family." A total of forty-eight roses filled my dressing room. My bridesmaids watched with envy. This demonstration of romance filled me with a profound sense of assuredness. Any doubt remaining was removed and the walk down — rather, the roll down the aisle — was made with pure excitement and great expectations.

As I gathered my thoughts and secretly prayed for the union I was about to enter, I laughed with joy as I remembered telling myself once before, *Now, Leslie in your situation you must be prepared to love an ugly man.* But, here I was, moments away from joining in marriage to a gor-

My father and I "roll" down the aisle.

Aaron carries me out of the church.

geous, masculine, handsome man who loved me just as I am. You see, when God answers a prayer He doesn't just do it half way. In this case, He went above and beyond the cry of my heart.

My wedding dress had been carefully fitted to my 5'3" frame. The dress had a beautiful pearl-beaded train. In order for the train to drape over the back of my wheelchair, I had to sit on several pillows to elevate my height. With a bouquet of white lilies, my father escorted me to the altar, where my mother joined us. Together, they gave me away.

Pastor Hicks shared stories of our love and facilitated the exchange of rings. We promised "to love and to hold, to cherish and honor, 'til death do us part." We kissed and were pronounced husband and wife. Aaron then leaned down and asked, "Are you ready, Mrs. Ostrander?" Then he smiled and picked me up. As he was carried me out of the sanctuary, my right shoe fell to the floor. I whispered, "It's just like Cinderella, even the lost slipper."

The wedding party followed our steps, and the only thing remaining at the front of the church was my empty wheelchair. My empty wheelchair, a symbol of the freedom I felt in the presence of Aaron. His willingness to accept my physical limitations as his own was a God-sent gift. I'm certain the culmination of his experiences and upbringing prepared him for our union. Aaron was the worthy partner I had prayed for. It was one amazing day! I was determined to make my life with Aaron one of happiness and success.

The groomsmen.

According to the Spinal Cord injury network, due to the youthful age of most persons with SCI, it is not surprising that the majority (51.6%) are single when injured. Among those who were married at the time of injury, as well as those who marry after injury, the likelihood of their marriage remaining intact is slightly lower when compared to the uninjured population. The likelihood of getting married after injury is also reduced.

After our marriage, my next priority was to focus on the upcoming Ms. America Wheelchair Pageant. I had been traveling the entire state and spoke to more than a thousand people through my journey as Ms. Wheelchair Georgia. Yet, I still found it difficult to share my story. I had grown up teaching myself to accept my disability, so when it came time to expose the reality of life in a wheelchair, I struggled to recreate the challenges I have to stare down daily. I come so accustomed to my life, that it was tough to discern those areas in my life that were different. That was, until I got married. Living in the same house with someone you deeply love brings with it a certain level of new challenges. But, when one of you is set apart by physical limitations, the terrain of the test can shift despite all positive reinforcement. What I'm trying to explain is that Aaron was a constant source of encouraging affirmation. However, I began to compare my life to his. The differences in my life were clear and easily recognizable.

My insecurities began to surface. If I allowed lack of confidence to overcome me, it could possibly come to the point where I may never leave my home. I had negative thoughts like, *You look so different. You are broken. It's just too difficult and exhausting to share my life with Aaron.*

I owe Aaron the credit for never allowing me to slip into this place of negatives. He has always treated me no different they he would anyone else. In fact, he often pushes and challenges me with tough love. In the first year of our marriage I think my immediate family had a problem with this. In their minds they thought my mate should handle me in only caring and sympathetic ways. Aaron's driven tactics to motivate me became an area of dispute. I knew his love…I experienced his love in a genuine way. I know it was only out of protection that my family might have questioned Aaron's objective. But in time they would all see that he was the right dose of enthusiasm I needed. If only everyone was as lucky to have an encourager like me.

When God calls us to be the salt and light, we are called to fulfill His purpose, despite our weakness, brokenness, and differences. God uses us the way we are. I march on in my marriage, as different as I may be, because I love the man I am with. I love the life we have created together and I simply refuse to let my disability cheat me from the riches that come from sharing life with my best friend. Aaron will have to answer for himself, but why he continues to see past my disability is truly a testimony of true love.

All Things are Possible through Jesus Christ

God alone does marvelous deeds. — Psalms 72:18

Aaron's background in adaptive sports brought to my life a new passion. I soon found myself in the water, skiing and tubing, in wheelchair racing, and off road four wheeling. I learned to draw motivation from our time together in sports and outdoor activities. By nature I'm not a thrill seeker. On the other hand, Aaron is almost obsessive when it comes to competitiveness.

My first attempt at wheelchair racing was out of unrelenting influence from Aaron. He just knew in his heart that I would be a successful racer. This sport was primarily dominated by men and there was a need for female participants. The sport was designed to match racers based on ability and strength. Athletes are classified by the severity of their disability. I would be racing females that had same or similar levels of injury. Since I was a high level quad there where few racers, elevating the likely hood of success.

Aaron became my coach. We spent time getting familiar with my high tech racer. The Soaring Eagle T- Frame V- Cage was fabricated from heat treated aluminum and was an apparatus designed for speed. Designed from the ground up for performance and velocity a competent driver was still a necessary component. If I was to thrive as a racer training was imminent.

A stationary trainer found an unoccupied space in our garage. A mirror was placed in front of the trainer. Watching my reflection allowed me to analyze my technique and strokes. I watched my army fly up and then felt the force in my muscles as they crashed down on the wheels.

"I'm jogging," looking up at my husband with a wry smile. Fifteen minutes - or six kilometers -later, I was ready to call it a day. My weathered appearance, in faded T-shirt and racing tights with flushed cheeks, was a remote look anything like the groomed and polished façade of my pageant days.

Despite all of my practice and weight training maneuvering the light weight racer proved to be harder than originally expected. As the days of training crept by and my muscles immersed in throbbing pain the anticipated race arrived. It was a 10K event located in the heart of Atlanta, Georgia. The southern sweltering heat in the middle of July was a concern for every athletic. Aaron had a plan.

He entered himself in the 10K. As with most races, the wheelchair division started first. Aaron's plan was to catch up with me. Positioned on his back would be a backpack sprayer. You know, those portable, automatic, air-compressed, hand-operated sprayers, used by agricultural professionals. Equipment that is ideal for professional *weed control*. The label on the hand sprayer read something like, "multi-purposes include garden spraying-weed and pest control, liquid fertilizing, plant leaf polishing, window-glass cleaning, wallpaper removing, and other applications used in agriculture and horticulture." No where did I read, "great for keeping wheelchair athletic cool and comfortable during 10K road race."

Although on lookers at the race must have been quite confused when they saw this man trailing me in a desperate attempt to hose me down, my husbands inventive idea was a brilliant innovation to combating the heat. I'm sure the other racers wished they were as fortunate. I was also the only person in my division. Therefore, all I had to do was finish to place. It might sound easy assuming I had no competition but it was a feat of determination to cross that finish line. I never found any lasting success in racing. It's a sport for the hard-wearing and resilient.

The cultured of wheelchair racing gave me the discernment to not be afraid to fail sometimes. For failure, after all, is what gives success it's great significance.

Two years into our marriage, we decided to take on a new kind of race. We explored our options of bearing children. Despite my injury, I had always had a deep-seeded desire to be a mother. I wanted to be prepared for all possible complications and physical changes. I had been told that

I could not bear children, primarily due to the traumatic stress it would put on my injured body. But, I had the call upon my life, that it was God's plan for me to be a mother. I also had convinced myself, that if I could not conceive, well, we would adopt. Somehow, I knew that I was meant to be a mother. I decided to take a team approach to my pregnancy, which would include my obstetrician and a physiatrist, a doctor specializing in rehabilitation medicine. To have a child of my own would certainly redefine my purpose. Motherhood was something I did not enter into carelessly. Scripture refers to motherhood as the highest calling a woman can have. I approached the possibility with extreme caution and placed it in the hands of Jesus Christ.

There were many uncertainties. Questions of how I would care for a child often entered my mind. I kept a journal of every fact and detail I could find. I learned that labor and delivery were natural processes and usually not affected by SCI. However, I was likely to experience some symptoms that are unique to SCI. These symptoms may include increased spasticity, autonomic reflexes, increased bladder spasms, and a problem with blood pressure spikes during delivery. There was some evidence that suggested that I may have a greater risk for premature delivery, prior to 36 weeks' gestation. It was a lot to consider. After several appointments, research, and countless hours of prayer, Aaron and I conclusively thought that pregnancy was a positive option for us. Like any other pregnancy, there were no guarantees. It took only two months for us to conceive. The next nine months would be an emotional experience; I had no idea of the dedication, and love that was forthcoming.

Nine weeks into my pregnancy, my obstetrician, asked me to come to her office for my first ultrasound. She greeted me with a smile. With Aaron's help, I lay down on an examination table. The nurse turned off the lights and the small room was illuminated by the screen on the sonogram. The doctor took the gel and lathered it across my belly. Then she placed the sensor on my abdomen; the womb appeared on the screen. Instantly, I felt deep love for this child. What a miracle.

It was then that I knew I would do everything within my power to ensure the health of my baby. I chose to limit my activities. I continued to build my upper body strength with daily exercise. My obstetrician carefully mapped out her expectations and discussed the things we would closely monitor throughout the next nine months. She instructed me to increase my fluids. My kidneys were already under stress due to my spinal cord injury, and a growing fetus was even more reason to frequently examine my kidneys.

I prayed continually. With each trimester came a new set of concerns and a new methodical plan of action. Each day I would envision the outcome, a beautiful, healthy child. I nourished my body with healthy foods and vitamins. Then one afternoon, deep inside my belly — a movement — it was like nothing I had ever felt before. I rejoiced in having the sensation. My level of injury had prevented me from feeling anything below my chest. For the first time, *I felt.* The movement from my unborn child was marvelous. With each passing day, the movements grew stronger and the baby became more active.

At six months' gestation, I decided I should take a leave of absence from work. It would be a small sacrifice, and the time off would help me prepare for the arrival of my firstborn. Aaron secured a second job in order to supplement our income. With a new baby on the way, our budget would be stretched thin. His time with me was limited, and we depended on the help of family and friends.

In the last weeks of pregnancy, most of my time was spent in bed. Braxton Hicks contractions became a familiar part of my day. The reoccurring tightening of uterine muscles was a good sign that my body was preparing for delivery. I prepared myself emotionally. I suppose other expectant mothers reach a point where they feel unmatched for the task ahead and are overcome with doubt and fear. I certainly did. I wondered if my desire to be a mother was something that was beyond my strength and capabilities. The delivery itself scared me. What would the weeks ahead bring?

I found escape from my concerns by relaxing in the baby's nursery. The pale yellow walls were cheerful, yet serene. The soft, plush animals my momma picked out were placed on a shelf that hung next to Aaron's baby quilt. A twin bed was next to the baby crib. The smell of baby powder, Desitin balm, and baby soap provided an inviting aroma. Whenever I was in the nursery, I would sit and sing softly to my womb, my favorite hymn, *He is There for You,* with my hand on my extended belly, feeling every movement of my unborn child.

Late one evening in February, I awoke to more contractions. The pregnancy made it difficult for me to successfully turn over in bed. Unable to see the alarm clock, I lay there and counted my contractions as my husband snored. The contractions were strong. Like a blood pressure cuff, the strain kept building, until I found it hard to breathe. I woke Aaron. Within minutes he was dressed, had the physician on the phone, and was ready to take me to the hospital. It was a cold winter night. An ice storm was forecast to hit sometime during the night. Aaron wrapped me up in multiple jackets. He so lovingly picked me up, placed me in the blue Toyota truck — the same truck in which we shared our first date — and we set out for the Medical Center. We said very little, except when timing my contractions. It was still five weeks until my due date, and we both were certainly worried that a delivery now would be too early. Although we did not speak of our fears, they were present like an unwanted guest.

The obstetrician was there to meet us. She could see I was in pain. We made our way to a room, where the nurses placed monitors along my belly. They inserted an indwelling catheter. The catheter itself was painful, the IV was extremely uncomfortable, and I shook with fear. Aaron took my hand and kissed my forehand; he illustrated his love when he said nothing at all.

"Leslie," the obstetrician said," We are going to try to get your contractions to slow down. If we can keep the baby in the womb for a few more weeks, our chances of a healthy baby will be increased." As she explained her plan of action, I quietly prayed. I felt every labor pain right down to the final screaming end.

Motherhood is the highest calling a woman can have. Motherhood is a gift. From the first sound of a baby's cry, to the first steps, to the first word, there's nothing as sweet as the presence of children. What do angels sound like? Listen closely to a child sing and you will hear an angel's voice. What does heaven look like? Look into a child's eyes to see the wonders of the heavens. What is peace? Hold a newborn baby in you arms and experience tranquility. I've heard the angels, I've seen heaven, and I've felt that perpetual bliss. When I first held Dylan, my first-born, I knew that I had found my purpose. I thank God for the gift of motherhood.

Simple Pleasures

Now the Lord is in the Spirit, and where the Spirit of the Lord is, there is freedom. — 2 Corinthians 3:17

"I've come to realize the importance to make time for you. If you don't recharge and nurture your passions, you run the high possibility of driving yourself into the ground-and then your life will go by too fast. The true content of life is then hard to recognize. I haven't always lived by this motto, but it's one that have adopted and embraced. I don't want to become one of those people who live to work. I want to work to live. I don't want to have a fulfilling life alone, I want to share each moment with someone I love."
— Actress, Jennifer Aniston

Clink. Clink, was the sound of our glasses as my sister and I toasted a great girls' weekend getaway in the glorious Floridian sun and blue skies. With a bag of chips, salsa and lemonade, we gazed at the emerald waters that lay before us. With our toe nails painted hot pink, in our faded denim shorts and our favorite tank tops, we vow to make this a yearly tradition. I love the sun, I love the sand, and I love the water. My sister shares the same love. As I take in this divine slice of tranquility, I realized that this beach was in a sense, a sacred place — a place far away from stress. I closed my eyes and ran my fingers through the coarse sand and imagined how it would feel to my feet. The warmth of the grains indulged my skin, and I buried my hands deep until the sand turned cool. I opened my eyes and glanced at my tan sister. She was quietly soaking up the warmth of the September sun. I enjoyed her company. We are all about doing "the girl thing": laughing, dancing, shopping, getting pampered, and enjoying the local tranquility of our favorite beach. I'm a lucky girl to have a friend in my sister.

This get-together was a new beginning for us. The spread of years be-tween our ages had always been an obstacle that put us in different places in our lives until now. We both had come to understand the importance of sisterhood. Her marriage to her supportive husband grounded her, and my growing family put demands on me that often required a need for her shoulder to cry upon.

My sister's wild spirit is often contagious. She reminds me life is short and that we should make time for the simple pleasures. "Leslie, you'd better have a blast in everything you do," my sister says, "Grab a hold to life and don't let go." She possesses the nerve and spirit of doing things spontane-ously, filling her life with fun and walking to the beat of her own drum. She is charismatic, overflowing with stories that are as juicy as ripe tomatoes.

You would never see her injury, but it's there. Physically she sustained no harm, but she was emotionally wounded. And although she has never spoken a word of her pain, I know it's there, every day. In many ways, it's a pain that is more difficult to deal with than mine. But, like her, I have learned that you get through things that hurt. My pain is real; my sister's pain is real. We never asked for it and we would never will it to any one else. It changed who we are. The human spirit is resilient and unbeliev-able. And through Jesus Christ, we find the strength and desire to push on and get the most out of every day.

Sisterhood is a cherished treasure for me. Most women have the luxury of asking a friend to go shopping. Something simple, with no strings at-tached. However, for me, the same situation is more complex. I fear that when I ask a friend, especially a new acquaintance, "Hey, let's go shop-ping," she will interpret this as, "Hey, come ride with me, help me up the ramp, reach that item on the shelf, chase my children, and then carry my purchases." For my friends who already have kids of their own, shopping with me and my two children — well, let's say it can be like a three-ring circus. I'm not suggesting that my friends make me feel this way; it's a source of my own insecurities. I know I'm loved and enjoyed, yet I feel as if I'm an added hassle in an already complicated world. Feelings like this require me to focus on my choices: To despise my disability and al-low it to hinder my social life, or to gratefully embrace it as a gift and go beyond my comfort zone.

Even though my disability is difficult to accept, I have found ways to see its purpose in my life. I had to first see my situation through the eyes of God. I still find it hard to make engagements with friends, yet I still do. I have learned that they too are nervous on first-time outings with me. But it is an experience that they grow from, taking with them a greater appreciation for the ease at which they can maneuver. After I openly share with them how they can assist me, they become more comfortable with future outings. It's a learning curve that all my friends must go through. That's exactly one of the many reasons I cherish the friend I have in my sister. Our sisterhood represents *freedom* for me.

Without saying a word, she aggressively jumps in where she is needed. Putting my shoes back on after I transfer from my car seat to my wheelchair. Adjusting my clothes, handing me my purse — we run like a finely tuned band, marching together toward the nearest "half-off" sale rack.

Whether I'm doing a school project with my five-year-old or staring down challenges of making new friends, I put forth the self-determination to leap into action to get the job done. I can't waste a minute not being happy or with self-pity. That will get me nowhere. Instead, I must focus on the great blessings and gifts that I do have: The servant friends God has provided and the unbreakable bond of sisterhood. In His Hands there is always freedom. Disabled or not, we all have the resources to be free!

For God so loved the world, that he gave his only begotten Son, that whosoever believeth in him should not perish and have everlasting life. — John 3:16

We are so valuable, that God sent His only Son to die for us. Because He places such value on us, we should never fear our trial and adversities. We are reflections of God's Awesome Glory.

It's not a crown; it's not a trophy or a degree of diplomacy that makes us possess great worth. Glamorous homes, luxury cars, and flawless diamonds are symbols that we have learned to value as wealth. And if you are not among the few who relish in these embellishments, we may feel envy, stress, or unworthiness. But do these things make us wealthy? Is the happiness we experience from material possessions fulfilling?

Don't get me wrong; I too, can't resist the sparkle of a diamond. I, too, read the home and garden magazines where executive homes are displayed. But aren't these subjects of entertainment? Or are they the things that *define our worth*?

I have found more enjoyable ways to define what really matters in my life. And if you make a list, you will soon realize that material objects rate low in the scheme of things. Friendship and the help of others have become a great importance to the quality of my life. It has been a long process for me to completely understand that asking for help is not a reflection of weakness. There is no purpose in soldiering through. Our relationships with others have greater purpose than enjoyment; taking pleasure in our friends is just an added bonus. I believe that our relationships are designed to nourish our constant need for companionship; God saw Adam and said, "This is not good," so he made Eve. It might seem trivial, but today it's easy to retreat to the privacy of our homes and avoid the awkwardness of meeting new people. We tend to think that we are fully capable of existing and tackling life's endeavors alone. There will come a time in everyone's life when they will be forced to ask for help. In fact, I believe asking for help is a sign of strength. To ask someone to enter into your life and assist in your needs requires trust, and trust is a tricky thing to give. Often trust and fear appear in the same moment. Fear sets in when the thought occurs to us that this person might let us down. But not asking a friend can deny you, as well as the friend, the purpose to which God has called us to do: "Love thy neighbor as you love thyself." God allows us to participate in his grand plan. We are called, not to sit back and watch God work, but to give our talents, resources, and self to the fulfillment of His plan.

Tirelessly, I often overextend myself refusing to ask for any help. As a child I witnessed my mother doing the same thing. Somehow I convinced myself that asking for help would dilute the meaning of my role as a mother.

After the birth of my son, my daily activities sweltered down to daily housekeeping. I wondered how doing the third load of laundry was within God's will. Had I become a glorified maid? Often I felt like I was operating in only a survival mode. A shower became a luxury. After months of exertion, I came to understand that I needed some assistance. My mother came to my rescue.

Molding Clay

Somehow the joy of a new baby seems to erase those nine months of pain. Aaron had expressed his wishes to try for a second baby. My first thought was, *Have you lost your mind?* In the midst of the terrible twos, another child was not open for discussion. The happiness Dylan had brought to us, however, made all rationalization irrelevant. Two years and three months after Dylan had been born, I was pregnant again.

My second pregnancy had been much like my first, until one hot summer afternoon in August.

We just returned from a family vacation at the beach. The weather was perfect. Dylan was tired from the trip and asked me to lie across the bed with him. I was twenty-one weeks gestation and took every opportunity to rest.

I drifted into an afternoon nap. When I awoke, I lay there and quietly watched Dylan, focusing on the gentle sound that he made as he inhaled then exhaled. He was so peaceful when he slept. I rolled onto my back and placed my hands on my slightly extended abdomen. I rubbed my hands over and around, praying for my unborn child. Then I noticed my belly; it felt different — harder. *Was this something I should be concerned about? Should I call the physician?*

After an hour of rest and no change in my tightened belly, I decided I should call

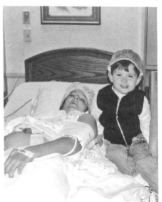

Just moments before I gave birth to Clay, Dylan's little face is filled with excitement. My face shows pain and distress.

my obstetrician. Dr. Cheek directed me to go to the hospital, where they could monitor for contractions. Contractions at twenty-one weeks? Is that even possible? With no hesitation, I drove myself to the hospital, leaving Aaron behind to care for Dylan.

I was greeted at the entrance of the hospital. A team of nurses had been informed that I was on my way. Within moments, they had monitors in place. A nurse stood over the machine marking the highs and lows on the paper stripe the machine was printing. "Mrs. Ostrander," she said, "how do you feel?" I replied, "I feel fine, just a little tired." She went on to inform me that I was, indeed, having contractions. In fact, my contractions were only minutes apart. Contractions this early in the pregnancy had to be stopped. "Will we be able to get the contractions to go away? If we can't, will the baby come early? Will the baby survive?" Without a single breath in between questions, I rambled on, tears welling up in my eyes and racing down my face. I looked at the nurse, practically begging for some reassurance that I was not about to have this baby. With the touch of her hand upon my shoulder, she simply said, "We are going to do our best to give that baby some more time. You'd better call your husband and let him know that you are going to be here for a while."

The team of nurses buzzed around me, something that seemed all too familiar. The head nurse explained a specific plan of treatment. Magnesium sulfate would be used to try to stop my contractions. A dose of corticosteroids would help speed up my baby's lung development. The contractions continued all day and all night. Around 2:00 a.m., a neonatal specialist came into my room. As gently as possible, he informed me that if my baby came this early the odds of survival were 50/50. He went on to say that the NICU (Neonatal Intensive Care Unit) was available and the specialists there could provide extensive care to improve these odds. The words were terrifying. This was my child we were discussing. Odds, 50/50 chance, specialist, survival...all these words, they were so impersonal, so horrifying. They just couldn't apply to me, or to my child.

After twelve hours of magnesium, I was hot, disoriented, and now paralyzed in over ninety percent of my entire body. It was difficult to open my eyelids. The intense strength that it took to breathe was suffocating. I was experiencing extreme respiratory depression, a serious side effect of the powerful drug. My will had been pushed to its limit. "Oh God," I cried out. "Why must I suffer? Why God, must my life be this difficult?" My spirit was broken. I was tired and I wanted to give up. For the first time in my life I found it hard to find the will to keep breathing. Had it not been for this unborn child, who I deeply loved, I would have wished for the end to be near. It was that horrific. I had been strong in the past. I had endured test after test. But this was too much. Why had God let me conceive this child if I was going to be too weak to deliver a healthy, full-term child? I felt like I was at death's door. Not even having enough energy to cry, I just lay there completely paralyzed.

The nurses encouraged me to get some sleep. I was afraid to sleep. If I fell asleep, I thought I would never wake up. Dr. Cheek entered the room. My mind responded quickly to his arrival, but my words came slow. My speech was slurred, my mouth was dry, and my voice was no more than a whisper. "Am I dying?" I managed to ask. He leaned toward me to understand my broken sentence and explained, "It's the magnesium. It's the side effects. Often times the "mag" causes muscle weakness; this can make you lose energy." I wanted to scream, "If the building was on fire, I couldn't even fall out of bed." I did manage to tell him that I knew I could not tolerate another round of magnesium. I was already scared that my next breath would not come. The good news was that the contractions had stopped.

I was restricted to bed rest from this point on. My family and friends saw it as a vacation from life. This could have not been further from the truth. I was now a woman trying to save her baby's life. Day after day, spiritual coping and emotional support was provided by my husband. He would make my breakfast, pack a lunch for me in an ice chest, and empty the indwelling catheter before leaving for work. Then he would take Dylan to daycare. After that, I was on my own. Using a monitoring device, I would record my uterine contractions, and via Internet they were closely watched by my team of physicians. Throughout the day, they would instruct me on appropriate dosages of medications to control the contractions. This enabled me to stay at home instead of being hospitalized.

As my belly grew and the baby became more active, the contractions became more frequent. Oral medication no longer worked, and Aaron was trained on how to insert an IV in my upper thigh. The medication was essential. Every three days Aaron would swab me with alcohol, pinch my skin, count to three and then insert the needle. After several weeks he became so comfortable with the process. I joked with him about taking his own frustrations out with each needle. We prayed together, we talked; we played games with Dylan — anything to pass the time. My occasional outing was once every two weeks, for a physician's checkup. It was in itself an all day affair. Aaron washed my hair with a small bucket and water pitcher beside my bed. He dressed me, changed my IV and picked me up to make the transfer to my wheelchair less strenuous. Once we made it to the doctor's office and back home, I was depleted. It would take me days to recover from the taxing day out. Any kind of activity made the baby more active, therefore sending me into more than eight contractions an hour. In my first pregnancy I felt terror. I never felt relaxed, so I needed reassurance. I found reassurance from friends. They did their best to keep me busy — if not my mind would return to thoughts of fear. This pregnancy was so different. There was too much time to ponder the negative possibilities.

Sometimes I felt resentful that the rest of the world continued on without me. Sometimes Aaron would go out with friends, saying he needed a break, but what about me? I was left alone. I felt selfish for feeling this way. Yes, Aaron deserved a break. I tried to be upbeat, but I battled depression. There was constant pain in my ribs and shoulders. My accelerated heartbeat, due to the medication, was strenuous. Then there was guilt; tremendous guilt that I was I neglecting Dylan, who now was three. The child I prayed for now was left to wonder why his mother could no longer care for him or play with him.

The only productive thing I could do was educate myself on preterm labor. The Internet became a resource. I began to understand that, as an informed patient, I was more confident and better able to advocate on behalf of my baby and my pregnancy. Weeks went by slowly. I was in and out of the hospital more than six times, sometimes staying in the hospital for more than two weeks.

While in the hospital, the physician would request routine ultrasounds. Each trip to the sonogram room would require my hospital bed to be strolled by the NICU. There, hanging upon the hallway walls, were black and white pictures of preemie babies. Some are smaller than an adult-sized hand, so sweet, so frail, and in the fight for their lives. I would secretly pray for my unborn child to escape the need for NICU. *Please, Jesus, give my body the strength that it needs to carry this child to full term.* I made a promise to Christ. If my child was born healthy, I would find a way to give back to the NICU. The NICU was an amazing place, a life-saving habitat, but one I hoped that we would elude.

At thirty-two weeks' gestation, I went to the hospital once more with contractions only a minute and half apart. With another round of medications, I was told that I would not leave the hospital until the baby could be delivered. For two more weeks, I completed my pregnancy in the company of a team of nurses, monitors, and ultrasounds. On December 5, 2003 Dr. Ben Cheek gave me the good news that the baby's lungs were fully developed. "You think you can round up the troops?" he said early in the morning, referring to multitude of family members who wanted to be present for the birth. I grinned slightly, tired and battered from the difficult pregnancy and replied, "They are already on stand by." Within what seemed like brief moments, compared to the agonizing four months of bed rest the doctor asked me to take a deep breathe. Then, I heard the cry of a newborn child. It was more like a scream! Instantly, love filled the room. We were blessed once again with a healthy boy. Although he was five weeks early, he weighed in at five pounds, seven ounces. He was a moose of a preemie! So often during those four months, I thought the

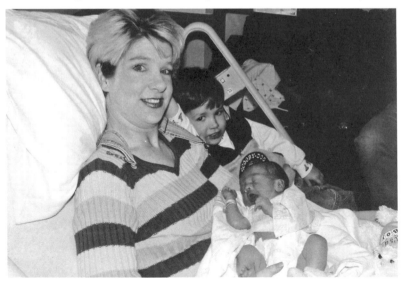

Two sweet blessings, Dylan and Clay.

103

little baby in the womb was like a piece of potter's clay that Jesus was shaping and molding into a beautiful child of His. It seemed fitting to name our new son, Clay.

The four months of pain, uncertainty, and fear seemed now like a mere second, a brief moment in the making of a miracle. Molding Clay had become a chapter in my life that was beautiful. The reward was so great. No pain, no bed rest was too insufferable for the joy I received in my new son. God had carried me through.

Parenting from a Wheelchair

When my children were babies I become so overprotective. I was so fearful that something would happen-*something horrible like what happen to me when I was young*. I watch them like a hawk. I secretly struggled to believe that I was capable in keeping the children safe. My trust in myself as well as my faith grew as I independently discovered my ability was adequate.

To watch my children grow is an experience that continues to keep me in awe. In just twelve short months, my children had gone from fragile newborns to busy explorers — getting into cabinets, crawling under beds, and putting small objects in their mouths. The children's rapid change was not easy for my slow pace. After weeks of trying to figure out a way to pick the children up and out of the playpen, days later they had figured it out for themselves and were crawling out on their own. When I learned how to efficiently change a dirty diaper in less than ten minutes, three days later they were ready to potty train. Somehow their skill and abilities quickly bypassed mine. I wondered, *Why Lord, do you give them so much energy and I am always tired. Why must they grow so fast?* On the other hand, I knew that their growth was necessary and that I was blessed to have such inquisitive children.

Parenting from a wheelchair is challenging, but possible. I've learned that much of my success depends upon careful scheduling and support from family and friends. I'm always thinking of ways to be more efficient. I discovered conventional baby items that are ideal for my situation: a bassinet on wheels, which I could steer from one room to another; and a nursing pillow, which I used for holding the children when they were infants. I could place the pillow on my lap and found it comfortable and safe for the children to use on the floor or bed.

I learned early on the importance of gaining their respect. I had to make them understand my authority. I'm not capable of physically controlling them; they both are stronger than I am. But when I speak, they know they'd better listen.

When I'm out shopping with the boys, they know to hold on to my wheelchair when crossing the parking lot. Oftentimes, my youngest will sit on my lap, as I push my wheelchair across the asphalt, and my oldest will hold tightly to the handlebar. The power in verbally telling the children what is expected of them and exactly how to accomplish a goal is the greatest asset to their safety.

The children help me in a thousand ways; from obediently crawling into their car seat to carrying packages. In the kitchen we keep all of our dishes in the lower cabinets in order that I can reach them, thus, putting them right within reach of my two-year-old. Anything I can reach is easily within Clay's grasp, making a child-proof home harder to achieve. With Dylan's help, we keep plastic dishes in the lower cabinets and glass items on the counters. Sometimes an object will get pushed to the back, preventing me from reaching it. Dylan will climb onto the counter and retrieve it for me. He has become a great helper. That's not to say that he is above taking advantage of the situation. Recently, when we went to the mall Dylan asked to go to the toy store. I said no, rather half-heartedly. He jumped from my lap and quickly took control of my wheelchair, pushing me right into the toy store. I laughed and allowed my strong-willed child to take pleasure in his favorite store.

As early as my children could comprehend, I began teaching them about their surroundings, taking every opportunity to tell them what was safe and what was harmful. "The stove is *hot*. Don't jump on the bed. This could *hurt* baby." I would map out areas in my home that we called "safe play." When the children were tempted to do something unsafe, I quickly pointed them to their "safe play" area.

Before Clay, my toddler, could even talk, he would fetch my wheelchair for me. Sometimes when transferring to my bed, I misjudge and tumble to the floor. First, Clay wraps his sweet arms around my waist and attempts to pick me up. As manly as a two- year-old can be, he grunts and makes every effort to pull me up. He watches everything. So many times he has seen Aaron pick me up from the floor. Often Aaron will theatrically grunt, implying that I am too heavy. Like father, like son. I have to convince Clay that his little muscles aren't strong enough. "Clay, thank you for helping Mommy; will you get me my wheelchair?" He then retrieves my wheelchair, which has rolled only a few feet away. I pull myself back into it and Clay claps his hands. He smiles with great accomplishment and returns to his usual play.

I didn't know whether to laugh or cry when I first noticed him, at nineteen-months-old, using his teeth to open the wrapping on his favorite cookies. It was an innocent imitation of me; he had seen me do this many times. Often using my teeth as tools, to replace the lost strength in my hands, Clay resorted to do the same. It just never occurred to him that he should just use his hands.

The children help out in a thousand ways-from obediently crawling into the safety car seats to carrying groceries. But that's not to say that they don't take advantage of the situation. We were at the mall recently and they both were pleading to go the toy store. They had their own money-which they had earned from helping me- and they desperately wanted to squander away their earnings. But I was in a rush. So I half-heartedly said no. Cleverly they dashed behind me and despite my willingness to control the wheelchair they muscled me right into the store. I had no choice but to stay and shop.

Children see my disability for what it is worth. Just like my boys, they understand that there is a difference in me, but they put little effort into seeing my limitations. A child will be the first to ask me, "Why are in you in a wheelchair?" Adults, however, will resist, and often tell their children that it's rude to ask. In my opinion, the straight forward question is as appropriate as asking "What is your name?" My disability is not shameful; it's nothing I can hide or wish to conceal.

As the boys get older, they become more independent. Dylan also knows how to respond to the questions of his peers. He will be the first to point out that his mommy can do almost anything — sometimes telling his friends that my legs are just rusty. Once he starts talking about swimming with me, fishing, and camping, his peers begin asking questions. Their curiosity changes into amazement. I have observed that my boys don't make a distinction between people with or without disabilities. I think this makes them more accepting and understanding of differences. It ultimately comes down to the way that it is perceived. I choose to see my injury through Gods eyes, as a gift. On the other hand, society perceives a wheelchair as weak, inferior, and as a symbol of brokenness.

Today, the Council on Social Development reports that about 9 percent of children under twelve "have a parent who is restricted in his or her activities because of health conditions." This equates to nearly 9 million parents with disabilities in the United States, or fifteen percent of all American parents. (Provided by the Looking Glass, an international resource for parents with disabilities)

SCI makes me become a master in finding new ways to get things done. Parenting is no different. Parents with SCI can manage a family. There are many different ways, resources, and support systems to help parents. Adaptive devices such as Velcro diaper covers and chest harnesses to carry newborns are available on several Web sites. Occupational therapists who work with persons with SCI can be a good source for developing techniques and can maximize your ability to care for your child.

Injured or not, parents commonly share parenting duties. For example, one parent might be responsible for bathing his or her child. This was one of Aaron's duties, while my daily responsibility was to feed and make playtime special. "Responsibility assignment" and honest communication allowed Aaron and me ways to uniquely use our talents and abilities.

I am well aware that there will always be individuals who believe that persons with SCI should be discouraged from becoming parents. It's difficult for the misinformed to understand that I can provide the essential needs for my children just as well as any mother. Those who assume that parents should never have to ask for help in caring for their children are obviously not realistic about parenthood. Asking for help and receiving it from others is a natural part of parenthood. It is very rare for parents to care for their child without any help from others. This fact is no different for parents with SCI.

The stress of parenting, housework, meal preparation, and supporting my husband in his career as a real estate professional quickly began taking its toll. Scoliosis-*curvature of the spine usually caused by long periods of sitting*-had set in years earlier. But the amount of time I was spending in my wheelchair had dramatically increased since the birth of my children. Lower back pain was beginning to hinder my activities. I strongly detested the way pain medication made me feel and it alone obstructed my ability to maneuver efficiently. I refused to take the narcotics that physicians recommended. Therefore I began to research alternative pain management for my condition.

I was intrigued when I discovered hot water therapy as a potential solution to my problem. Hydrotherapy historically had been used as treatment of a variety of diseases, including arthritis and bone disorders. There were positive benefits for people with quadriplegia and scoliosis. But my excitement was hampered when I researched further the cost of hot tubs. My insurance would not reimburse for hydrotherapy at a physical therapy clinic nor would they cover the cost of a personal hot tub. Hydrotherapy is not a *"proven"* source of pain management, therefore a non-reimbursable item for health care providers. The cost of a hot tub was far exceeding our family budget and I dismissed the idea.

Months later, Aaron came home from work and told me that the next night he was taking me out on a date. He had already arranged for my mom to watch the children and even said that I should shop for a new outfit. *What a treat!* It had been a while since we had a date night and I welcomed the quite personal time shopping.

The next day I spent meandering through the sales rack and enjoying a quite lunch. When it came time for Aaron to take me on our date, he took my hand, "You trust me, don't ya?" It had been eight years since we had been married and I fount it humorous that he still had the need to ask me if *I trusted him.* I responded by asking, "Should I?" In this moment, like times before, he maintained a sense of mystery. What was he up to?

He smiled with an alluring sense of assurance. He pulled from his pocket a bandanna. "A blind fold," he said, "we must not ruin the surprise." Here I was almost a decade into marriage and two kids later and I had that same feeling that had cropped up in my heart when he had surprised me with the horse drawn carriage. I did not dare ask him where we were going. He had gained my trust many years before and had proven that most of his surprises worked out to be delightful. I graciously allowed him to blind fold me and placed my hand in his. He rolled me into our modified van and he assisted me with my transfer to the passenger seat-I had never tried this before with a blindfold.

The car ride took more than ten minutes and I desperately attempted to map out in my mind the turns and roads that we were traveling on. But my efforts were futile as I a have a horrible sense of direction. Blindfolded my bearings were truly inverted.

Once we had reached our final destination, Aaron placed me in my wheelchair, rolled me into what seemed like a store-*the bell on the door was my clue*- he removed the bandanna and my eyes readjusted to the sight of a showroom full of hot tubs and saunas. With confusion in my eyes, Aaron replied, "The store closes in five minutes, I have arranged for a private test soak to try out the hot tubs." It was one of those *AHH* moments. You know where your heart sinks down into your stomach and the thought alone makes time and space disappear. Yes…he had done it again.

Despite the high cost of the Hot Spring tubs Aaron explained that he was dead serious on me getting the benefits from hydrotherapy. It was my health that was his main concern and the expense of the tub was secondary. He insisted that we try out every tub until we found the perfect match for me to comfortably relax.

Now Aaron knew that I would have never agreed to do a test soak during normal business hours. The thought of strangers seeing me in my bathing suit-*although I had been in a swimsuit years ago in front of an audience*- terrified me; my years had brought me more modesty. And since this had been a surprise, Aaron had packed a bag with my swim attire. The only regret I had was the amount of time I had primped and manicured my hair.

We spent more than an hour talking and soaking in those tubs. At the end of our visit we had selected a hot tub that would be delivered the next day. My pain from the scoliosis soon became a memory of the distant past and my romantic story of how I came to be the proud owner of a Hot Springs tub makes most women green with envy.

Life often provides situations where we are given a chance to be grateful in the love we receive from others. The emotion created when someone shows their love is like no other. Yet, we must not look to others for our happiness. "…in thy presence is fullness of joy" (Psalm 16:11). I watched my momma strive to meet every need of my father. I watched her as she relentlessly looked for him to provide every aspect of her happiness. She spent a lifetime searching for validation, allowing her self-worth to be defined by her husband. She built her life around him. After twenty-five years of marriage my parents divorced. It was heart wrenching for me as I had always looked to both my mother and father for support. After divorce, my momma had to find her way in life. She undeniable had her moments where she felt overwhelmed and alone; depression was a reoccurring emotion and often times the memories of her past were greater than the dreams of her future.

My momma is a strong woman. She found strength in Christ to carry on after tragedy and even divorce. I think she always saw that God's assignment for her life was to be a caregiver. I hope that I have learned through her experiences that love is a gift. That there are no guarantees in love, yet we can't let the uncertainty of the future keep us experiencing the courtship of loved ones.

Are you dealing with negative emotions? Do you allow the past to hold you back? I'm sure my momma would give you this helpful advice, "Just spend a few quite moments with God. Experience Him with a fresh awareness. Get into His presence. I assure you that a hearty serving of Jesus is just what the doctored ordered. It's the best home remedy for depression there is. It will absolutely change your attitude and your life."

Sweet Angelic Voice

"Come here, son. I'm going to tickle you." As my son and husband played in the floor, I remembered when he was just a five-pound baby — so dependent, with a cry that was too weak to be heard in the next room. Now, a bustling five-year-old, the whole house was stirred by his laughter and strong voice. "Daddy, I'm stronger than you are. Watch me." *Bam!* Then a violent scream! He had fallen off the footstool and hit his head on the coffee table. I wheeled to him, picking him up; my husband quickly placed his hand on Dylan's forehead. Blood streamed out.

"Here, take him. I'll get some ice!" I said. Within moments, our nice night at home was interrupted with a moment of terror. To see your son in pain is a fearful, heart-stopping experience. I passed the ice to Aaron and found the number to the nearest emergency room.

Aaron would have to drive him there. If he needed stitches, there would be no way for me to control him when his own fear set in. I would stay behind to watch after Clay and would pray that the care for Dylan's cut would only be minor. I made myself wait long enough for them to get to the ER before placing my first phone call to Aaron's cell phone. "Has the doctor seen him yet?" I asked. "Yes, he's here right now. Looks like he will only have to use liquid stitches," Aaron informed me.

"Great. Let me speak to Dylan," I asked. "How do you feel, Buddy?" And with the sweetest angelic voice you have ever heard, he replied, "Mommy, I wish you were here." My heart fell deep into my chest. Speechless, I just prayed, "Thank you, Jesus, for letting me be a mother."

Maybe Reese Witherspoon put it best in her acceptance speech of her first Oscar for Walk the Line. She said, "I'm just trying to matter." Just a small town Southern girl from Tennessee, she went on to say that she was trying to do work that made a difference in the lives of others. Or perhaps it was best put in the Rascal Flatts top hit, *Bless the Broken Road:*

It's all part of a grander plan that is coming true…

This much I know is true
That God blessed the broken road
That led me straight to you.

I've walked the broken road that lead me to love, purpose, and life. Thank God for my broken body that ultimately made me whole. The days in ICU, the four months of bed rest during pregnancy, forced me to look up.

My greatest fear was not being able to find my place in this world, that my injury had robbed me of my destiny. Instead, it positioned me on a course where I cultivated strength and considerable integrity.

I can say with confidence that on August 17, 1979, in that day among twisted metal and glass shards. A day that started out ordinary ended tragically. On a sweltering hot, asphalt two lane country road, God was there. God was in control. I know this because of the providence of God — the foresight and the arrangement of all events to accomplish God's purpose for my life.

My injury has taught me valuable lessons. And loss itself is what pointed me in the right direction. If I had not been disabled, would mine and Aaron's paths have crossed? Would I have found my soul mate? Would I be the person I am now?

A friend of mine, Pam Baker once said, "Leslie I see you embracing your entire life, filled as it is with lumps of both sugar and vinegar as a gift from God." Sweet and sour as they may be, the gifts in life, sometimes unwanted, are equal parts of who we are. In time we will discover that it is our choice of reception that determines our satisfaction in life. We will be rewarded with things eternal for our sufferings and disadvantage. It's more than just discovering the silver lining. It is turning a life wrenching moment into an ambitious, life-altering plan. It's knowing that we are always In His Hands.

Blessed is the man who perseveres under trial, because when he has stood the test, he will receive the crown of life that God promised to those who love him. When tempted, no one should say, 'God is tempting me.' For God cannot be tempted by evil, nor does he tempt anyone.
— James 1:12-13

One day I hope to hear Him say, "Well done, my good and faithful servant. Come and share my happiness!" Oh what a glorious day that will be.
—Leslie

Final Thoughts

What will you do when adversity shows it's ugly face at your door? What would you do if you saw a tractor trailer in your lane of the road? I'm certain that your life too would never be the same.

If I had the power to choose, would I want to be paralyzed? Would you like to be disabled? Doubtful…I don't think so. I can't imagine anyone who would deliberately choose brokenness. And I would be a liar if I said that I would choose the same path of adversity. There are days that I still struggle to find the strength to muscle through-but somehow I do. I march on grasping hope closely to my heart.

Hope allows anyone to change from within. How does a child raise above misfortune to claim a life of happiness? How does a paralyzed woman face down the challenges of parenting from a wheelchair? There is no other explanation than the love of Jesus Christ. A God appointed assignment, encumbered with physical inadequacies, wealthy with freedom, only made possible by the power of God.

There will come a time in everyone's life where they will face crossroads. Answers to problems, solutions to heart ache will sometimes be hard to find. Disability or not we will all recognize the limits to our power. The healing power of Christ will prove to be the only lasting solution that will make all things new. *"Therefore if any man be in Christ, he is a new creature: old things are passed away; behold, all things are new" (2 Cor 5:17).* Spiritually, psychologically, emotionally, and relationally we have the need for restoration.

Where ever you are in your life, what ever the circumstance may be, I encourage you to experience God in a real and personal way. It doesn't take a wealth of knowledge just a heart that desires to be transformed and cleansed of sin.

That is the sole purpose of sharing my story. This books conception has been a healing and liberating experience personally. My journey of recapturing memories and revisiting painful moments has reassured me that I have always been in His Hands. It would be impossible to separate my story from the living word of God. That's not to say that I always realized the presence of Christ; it's a realization I've come to know as I understand His awesome grace.

In the midst of loss, death, and brokenness, God still gave me an abundance of reasons to live, three of which I shared in this story: my marriage, the birth of my children, and my passionate love for Jesus Christ. Had I given up when my life was changed by paralysis, I would have never known these great joys.

I gratefully accept the trials and tribulations that have made me become the woman I am today-for my adversities have made a woman of substance. To share my story with you is an honor; it was presented for your entertainment, but it is my hope that you found my experiences to be uplifting and motivating in your personal life.

To my fellow friends with disabilities, often I have turned to you to share my fears, pain, and joy. It is always refreshing for me to be among friends who understand firsthand the daily struggles of life with a disability. Many of you have aspired and achieved greater things than I. There is a unique and personal story that every one of you represent; each respectively shares a sense of loss, pain, survival, and rising above. And there are so many of you that have a positive perspective on life. Like my friend David Ring. He travels the nation, sharing with anyone that will listen, the joys he has found in life. Facing the challenges of cerebral palsy, he is fearless when he boldly confesses his love for Jesus Christ. He puts it so well. In his words he shares with audiences that hang on his every word.

He explains, "I have learned a deep truth. The truth is that everything works together. Everything we have gone through and will go through in our lives, good or bad, is for a purpose. When I applied that to my own life, I realized that I was born with Cerebral Palsy to further the gospel of Christ." If we could all be as fortunate as David! Stricken with a life of hardships, he is a man that knows the purpose of his life. He puts his whole heart into God's hands and he, by far, one of the most remarkable, happy people I have know.

Health and Beauty are Inseparable

Do you not know that your body is a temple of the Holy Spirit, who is in you, whom you have received from God? You are not your own; you were bought at a price. Therefore honor God with your body.
—1 Cor. 6:19-20

How do you really feel about yourself? When negative thoughts enter your life where do you turn to seek the truth?

God created you in His image. He knows you better than you know yourself. The only place to seek truth in life is through Christ and His amazing love. When you seek and see the truth you will naturally live faithfully and beautifully!

It is important to adopt healthy lifestyles. We must make positive choices in life that will help cultivate the basic value of our body as a temple for God. It's also a proven fact that the healthier you are, the better you look. Want to be beautiful? Then live a healthy lifestyle. Start with the inside. Learn to love yourself. Your talents, spiritual gifts, and natural beauty will shine through if you allow yourself to discover the real you. Look into the mirror and see the jewel that Christ made. Any child of God is beautiful; we just have to embrace the likeness in ourselves.

Here are a few of my favorite health tips:

Move More

Make it a personal challenge to find ways to move your body. Obviously I can't climb stairs if given a choice between that or elevators. However, I can push my wheelchair while taking the dog for a walk. I can toss a football with friends, and if I my husband can find a way to make the riding lawn mower adaptive with hand controls, I'm certain I will be mowing the lawn. Anything that moves your limbs is not only a fitness tool; it's a stress-buster. Consider motion in small increments throughout your day. It doesn't require an hour in the gym or a forty-five-minute aerobics class. For the busy mom or the professional on the go, just move more.

Cut Fat

Everyone knows that our diets should contain little fat. But it's sometimes difficult to become a mean, lean fat-burning machine. Keep it simple. Avoid the obvious fast food restaurants. It's all about choice. Think about it. Basic, good, wholesome choices, whether in diet or life, are the foundation of a healthy and fulfilling life.

Reduce Stress and Adopt a Positive Attitude

Easier said than done. Stress-busters come in many forms. Experts suggest that positive thoughts are a key source of relieving stress. Spend thirty minutes each day doing something for yourself. My favorites: a soak in a hot tub with aroma therapy candles; reading an inspiring book; visiting a friend; listening to uplifting music; have a good laugh. Remember to pamper yourself. Get a massage, a facial, or a new haircut. Surround yourself with people who support and motivate you.

Researchers of positive psychology have found that people with positive attitudes are happier, healthier, and live longer than those with negatives attitudes and habitual negative thinking. Avoid difficult people when possible. Surround yourself with people who will encourage you. But when stress shows it's ugly face remember it's how we choose to deal with our stressors that ultimately will define the way we shape our lives.

Wear Your Seat Belt!

I'm a living testimony of how important it is to wear your seatbelt. It's simple, easy, and only requires a few seconds out of a driving trip. Once you start to buckle up, it will become routine. No one is immune to a spinal cord injury. Since 2000, motor vehicle crashes account for 46.9 percent of reported SCI cases. The number one cause of SCI is automobile accidents. The next most common cause of SCI is falls, followed by acts of violence (primarily gunshot wounds). If you take away anything from his book, let it be this: Buckle Up and be familiar with your surroundings!

Drink Plenty of Fluids

Chronic bladder infections and kidney diseases are constants in a spinal cord injury survivor's life. Catheters contribute to high infection rates. The best defense we have is to drink plenty of fluids, especially water. My daily water regimen begins with three concentrated cranberry pills; studies show that cranberry juice helps maintain and promote a healthy urinary tract. Antibiotics are sometimes required for SCI, but this is determined by your physician. Routine checkups and annual renal ultrasounds should be a part of any SCI health plan. Injury or no injury, drinking water just makes good sense!

Frequently Asked Questions

About my children

Are your children adopted?
No, my boys are 100 percent mine. A pure gift from God.

Did you give natural childbirth?
No. I elected to have a cesarean section. Along with my obstetricians, we all decided that due to the lack of abdominal muscles, this would work best for my situation.

Was it difficult for you to care for an infant?
The early baby days, from birth to about six months, were the most challenging days. Feedings every two hours, frequent spit-ups requiring multiple clothing changes, and the fragility of a newborn provided me with obstacles. But through creative thinking, I was able to adapt ways to care for my boys with little to no assistance.

How do you manage a defiant toddler?
Thank God for patience! A defiant toddler can be a task for any mother and for my six year old, this is usually an every day occurrence. I try to be consistent with my discipline.

Just for Fun

What is your favorite family outing?
I enjoy any activity with my family. But my favorite is going boating and deep-sea fishing with my husband and children.

Who are your favorite actors?
Mel Gibson, Tom Hanks, Mathew McConaughey

In His Hands: Reclaiming Your Life After Tragedy

Who are your favorite actresses?
Susan Saradon, Jennifer Aniston, Reese Witherspoon

Who are your favorite musicians?
Michael W. Smith, Joey McIntyre, Nat King Cole

What are your favorite books?
The Bible, The Notebook, Message in a Bottle

What are your favorite movies?
The Passion of the Christ, Shall We Dance, Forrest Gump
(my favorite part, of course, is "Run Forrest, run!")

What's your favorite family experience?
Sharing a morning cup of coffee. My mother in law calls it "our morning meeting." My father sips his coffee with his beloved dog, Puggy, in his lap. Whatever the case, there's something magical in sharing a cup of java with people you love.

What's your favorite food?
Japanese Steak house, Sushi, and strawberries (but not at the same time).

Let's get Personal
What are your long-term goals?
To raise my children to be Christian, respectful gentlemen, attend as many public events where I can encourage others to be confident and self-motivated. Write a daily devotional manual and land a gig as a radio/television host on a Christian or motivational program. I have the need to utilize mainstream media to foster awareness.

What are your short term goals?
To get my eight year old through third grade; it will take a lot of prayer.

What are your favorite keepsakes?
My pictures of my children and my grandmother's antique china cabinet are very dear to me.

What types of modifications have you made to your home?
The underside of the stove, sink and kitchen counters are carved away so I can roll my wheelchair close. This helps me with preparing the meals for my family. It also protects me from dangerous spills. A front-load washer and dryer keeps laundry at a workable level-although I am great about delegating this chore to my husband. The door ways in my home are wider and I had a roll in-shower in stalled. I also have a ramp van especially equipped with hand-controls.

Who is the woman in the Bible you most relate to?
Hannah, just an ordinary woman who wanted to have children. She was devoted and set her heart on heavenly things. She made the promise to dedicate her son to the Lord. She experienced a lot of disappointment and heartache before Christ answered her prayers. She was never a complainer. Her trials made her stronger in her faith and prayer. Hannah's was steadfast. She believed God, in His own time, would answer her prayers. Like Hannah, I believe that motherhood is the highest calling God can bestow upon a woman. As a mother, I also feel the great responsibility to raise my sons to live for Jesus Christ and pray they will love Christ as He first loved us.

What has been your greatest self-confidence builder?
Competing and placing in the Miss America Preliminary Pageant. The experience of competing with able-bodied women was liberating and powerful. My objective in entering the pageant was to prove that inner beauty accounts for a lot more than the face value it's often given. Inner beauty, combined with self-confidence, in my opinion, is what makes a woman sexy and beautiful.

Whom do you hope gets inspired by this book?
My family. Often the people that are the closest are the ones that don't fully understand the scope of my struggles. It's important for them to understand that it is by grace, not my will, that I have succeeded. "This is the day the Lord hath made, we should be glad and rejoice in it." Let's give credit where credit is due.

What gets under your skin?

Excuses! Excuses are for people who have little commitment and determination. And complaining! No matter how bad you think your situation is, there is always someone who is worse off. I speak across the nation and educate audiences how to achieve lofty goals. Step one, always is to eradicate excuses.

What has been your most memorable speaking engagement?

Victory Baptist Church in Searcy, Arkansas; it was the first time that David Ring and I teamed together to share our testimonies. He had never head me speak before and was taking a huge leap of faith by extending the invitation. It was a remarkable event and people were moved to laughter and tears. This speaking engagement was the mark of a new chapter in my ministry.

I will also never forget providing the keynote speech at the annual state convention for Safe Kids, a national, federally funded program. The event was held at the University of Georgia in Athens. My job was part educational and part motivational. I strongly support Safe Kids. Nationally they have many projects. Among them is inspecting children's car safety seats and helping to provide them for people who can't afford them.

It seems that each time I speak there is an element that makes each speaking engagement memorable. The people I meet, the places I go. Each time I'm in front of people sharing, I always think what an awesome experience it is.

What do you do when you seem inclined to focus on the negative parts of your disability?

Positive affirmation always helps me. I have developed a sharp awareness of my accomplishments and purpose in life. I remind myself of these things daily. This helps me to nip negative thinking in the bud before it escalates. Learning to question and re-structure your thinking when it turns negative can help anyone think positively. It's like breaking a bad habit. One must see themselves as a conqueror. It takes work but the benefits are well worth it.

Do you think a cure is on the horizon?
Absolutely! It's more than optimism. It's recognizing the advancements in medicine I've witness as a Spinal Cord Injury survivor. In my twenty nine years as a quadriplegic there have been advancements in all areas. Rehabilitation has improved. Funding is recognized as a chief component- although there is a need for more. Quality of life is better, which seem to be byproducts of the search for a cure.

However, I'm a huge advocate of not waiting for cure…but living until the cure is cultivated. Having hope for a cure is something beyond the illness. Dedicating one self to living, rather than waiting, automatically puts emphasis on living life. I carry with me the hope of a cure while experiencing life to its fullest.

What is the biggest misconception regarding your injury?
People often mistake me as a paraplegic. They see only the wheelchair and my stone still legs, but see the movement in my arms. But C-7, quadriplegic, incomplete is quite different. Not being able to walk is slightly more than an inconvenience, it's the things that come with paralysis that humbly require endurance.

What is the best advice you can give to someone in midst of a hardship?
Get on your knees and pray! Do not make any major discussions when you are walking in a valley. Wait until you are back on top in order to make a clear and sound judgment. Tell yourself everyday that the adversity you are starring down is temporary. Although difficulties can seem absolute…any circumstance holds the potential for improvement. In time I'm sure that things will and can improve.

How do you explain Jesus to your children?
I try to demonstrate Christ-like qualities for my children daily. I pray with them. I talk about Jesus. I live my life based on the principles of faith. I show my children love and Christ is love! They are receptive and eager to understand God's unconditional love.

Therefore I tell you, do not worry about your life, what you will eat or drink; or about your body, what you will wear. Is not life more important than food, and the body more important than clothes?

Who of you by worrying can add a single hour to his life? So do not worry, saying, `What shall we eat?' or `What shall we drink?' or `What shall we wear?'

For the pagans run after all these things, and your heavenly Father knows that you need them.

But seek first his kingdom and his righteousness, and all these things will be given to you as well.

Therefore do not worry about tomorrow, for tomorrow will worry about itself. Each day has enough trouble of its own.

Oh my dear friends, God is always in control.

— Leslie

Acknowledgements

Thank You Jesus for Your grace, for Your unfailing love, and Your presence in my life.

I pray that this book will be used for Your divine purpose. Aaron, your dedication to my dreams and continual encouragement, acceptance, and unconditional love amaze me every day. You are more than I could have ever hoped for. Most of all, thank you for allowing me to be the mother of our two precious boys. Truly they are Gifts from God! To my dearest Dylan, you provide me with the strength to continue on. Your helpful, gentle spirit is contagious to those around you. You will not understand the depth of my love until you have your own first born. Clay, my miracle baby, who stole my heart even after four months of a painful pregnancy, I would do it all again, ten times over, just to see you smile. God gave you a gift of joy and passion for laughter and fun. I know you will share that gift. My two boys, you gave me purpose, you made me feel needed, and I will always be there for you. The greatest gift has been to be your mommy.

To my momma, it has been tough but we have done great things, especially when we worked as a team. I treasure our friendship; I value your support, and will forever be indebted to you for teaching me the importance of grace, poise, and womanhood. You are an amazing mother and an extraordinary friend. Dear dad, I will always draw strength from your ability to see past the obstacles. You always found a way to include me, and your refusal to expect nothing less has made me push myself beyond my greatest expectations. Sister, you have made me laugh, you have made me cry. And at times you have made me scream. But most of all, you have made me realize the joy of having a best friend in a sister. Brittany, you too are like a sister; I just wish you would have never grown up. You will always be dear to me and I will hold tight to the days we have shared together; my prayers are always with you.

To my Ostrander family, they always say you can pick your husband but can't pick your inlaws. Well, maybe that's true, but I couldn't pick anyone better. Bonnie, you have cared for me in times of sickness. You have listened to me cry and complain. I am certain that God not only chose my husband, but saw you as a person who would fill many needs in my life. Rex, your kind, Christ like spirit leads by example; often a quiet man, you convey your love in the commitment you demonstrate to your family and friends. Thank you both for raising such an outstanding son. Alexis, you have a life of opportunity ahead of you. Grasp each day with ambition and prayer. Jason and Christy, your love for Christ and dedication to His purpose is a blessing. I am glad my children can be surrounded by the love of a Christian family.

Ginger and Big MeMe, you are a part of this crazy extended family. I am grateful that you have always opened your hearts to me. Thank you for encouraging me to reach for my dreams.

To my church family who has given endless love. Bethesda is a wonderful place to be and the presence of Christ is felt each time I fellowship there.

To my physicians who have kept me healthy. Dr. Ronald Hudson, Dr. William Harper, Dr. Phillip Schley, Dr. Cynthia Fernandez, Dr. Ben Cheek, Dr. Richard Wilson, Dr. Charles Scarborough, and countless others; thank you for your wisdom and skills.

David Ring, thank you for having faith in me. Your friendship is an absolute gift. You are a mentor and treasured jewel for all. Thank you for giving me a platform and opportunity to share the stage with you. Thanks for making the time to invest in helping my ministry grow. Your eeternal rewards are well deserved.

There are so many people who have given me the resources, support, or kind words to fulfill the dream of writing this story. To each and every one of you who has ever believed in me, I am forever grateful! I have a wonderful life and it has been made wonderful because I am surrounded by amazing people. My success is your success! We are all *In His Hands*. Thank you. I love you.

If I would I have given up on life, look at the great blessings I would
of missed out on. Life is a gift!

Leslie and her husband while they were dating

Leslie and her bridesmaids

Leslie Ostrander and David Ring